MW00603421

CONTRACT TYPES

FEDERAL PUBLICATIONS SEMINARS

NATIONAL CONTRACT MANAGEMENT ASSOCIATION

FEDERAL
PUBLICATIONS
SEMINARS

PART OF THOMSON REUTERS

TABLE OF CONTENTS

TABLE OF CONTENTS

TABLE OF CONTENTS

UNIT 01

CONTRACT TYPE SELECTION

Contract Types

I.

Agencies have broad discretion in determining the contract type that is most appropriate for each requirement. One of the major functions of each contract type is to allocate risk between the parties. Under some contract types (e.g., firm fixed price) the contractor bears all risk of cost increases; whereas under other contract types (e.g., cost plus fixed fee), the government bears the risk of cost increases. The type of contract (i.e., cost reimbursement, fixed price, time and materials, etc.) has a direct effect on the monitoring of costs, the billings under the contract, and the cost and pricing considerations in proposing and negotiating a contract. The decision of which contract type to use should be based on an assessment of the risks, the complexity of the requirement, the ability to accurately predict costs, and the level of competition in the marketplace.

II.

The *Federal Acquisition Regulation (FAR)* provides an overview of the issues involved in selecting contract types:

16.101 General.

(a) A wide selection of contract types is available to the [g]overnment and contractors in order to provide needed flexibility in acquiring the large variety and volume of supplies and services required by agencies. Contract types vary according to (1) the degree and timing of the responsibility assumed by the contractor for the costs of performance, and (2) the amount and nature of the profit incentive offered to the contractor for achieving or exceeding specified standards or goals.

(b) The contract types are grouped into two broad categories: fixed-price contracts (see subpart 16.2) and cost-reimbursement contracts (see subpart 16.3). The specific contract types range from firm-fixed-price, in which the contractor has full responsibility for the performance costs and resulting profit (or loss), to cost-plus-fixed-fee, in which the contractor has minimal responsibility for the performance costs and the negotiated fee (profit) is fixed. In between are the various incentive contracts (see subpart 16.4), in which the contractor's responsibility for the performance costs and the profit or fee incentives offered are tailored to the uncertainties involved in contract performance.

III.

FAR 16.103(a) provides that the objective is to negotiate a contract type and price (or estimated cost and fee) that will result in reasonable contractor risk and provide the contractor with the greatest incentive for efficient and economical performance. Section 16.103(c) notes that during an acquisition, changing circumstances may make a different type appropriate, and states that contracting officers should avoid protracted use of cost-reimbursement or time-and-materials contracts after experience provides a basis for firmer pricing.

IV.

FAR 16.104 identifies some of the factors that the contracting officer should consider in selecting the contract type:

A. Whether price competition is available,

B. Accuracy of price or cost analysis,

C. Type and complexity of the requirement,

D. Urgency of the requirement,

E. Period of performance or length of production run,

F. The contractor's technical capability and financial responsibility,

G. Adequacy of the contractor's accounting system,

H. Concurrent contracts,

I. Extent and nature of proposed subcontracting, and

J. Acquisition history.

V. STATUTORY RESTRICTIONS

A. A statutory prohibition against cost-plus-percentage-of-cost (CPPC) contracting is found at 10 U.S.C. § 2306(a) and 41 U.S.C. § 254(b), and is implemented in FAR 16.102(c). In general, a contractual provision is prohibited if it assures the contractor of greater profits if the contractor incurs greater costs. The criteria used to identify a proscribed CPPC system, as enumerated by the court in *Urban Data Sys., Inc. v. United States*, 699 F.2d 1147 (Fed. Cir. 1983) (adopting criteria developed by the comptroller general at 55 Comp. Gen. 554, 562 (1975)), are

1. Payment is on a predetermined percentage rate,

2. The percentage rate is applied to actual performance costs,

3. The contractor's entitlement is uncertain at the time of award, and

4. The contractor's entitlement increases commensurately with increased performance costs.

A. The prohibition on cost-plus-percentage-of-cost contracting goes back to the 1940s, and is a reaction against its widespread use and abuse by World War I contractors. It is viewed as a "negative incentive" arrangement, since the contractor is arguably penalized for efficiency and rewarded for inefficiency.

B. In addition, annual appropriates and authorization acts may limit use of certain types of contracts. See, for example, the restriction on the use of cost-plus-fixed-fee contracts implemented in DFARS 216.306(c).

VI. REGULATORY LIMITATIONS

A. Sealed bid procedures. Only firm-fixed-price contracts or fixed-price contracts with economic price adjustment may be used under sealed bid procedures. (FAR 16.102(a) and 14.104.)

B. Competitive negotiation. Any contract type or combination of types described in the *FAR* may be selected when using competitive negotiations. (FAR 16.102(b).)

C. There are limits on the use of fixed-price Department of Defense (DOD) research and development (R&D) contracts. (DFARS 235.006.)

D. Only firm-fixed-price contracts, fixed-price contracts with economic price adjustment, and certain types of time-and-materials contracts may be used for commercial items acquisitions. (FAR 12.207.)

VII.

The remainder of FAR Part 16 includes guidance on the circumstances in which the individual contract types are applicable, and some prerequisites to the use of certain contract types. These prerequisites include the adequacy of the accounting system, the system's ability to determine allocable and allowable costs, and the existence of reliable historical cost data to use in determining a fair and reasonable price and in properly allocating risk. In the following sections, various contract types will be identified and described so that practitioners will be better able to select the contract type that is most appropriate for a given situation.

UNIT 02

Basic Contract Types

Contract Types

I. Introduction

A. Contract types vary according to

    1. The risk and responsibility assumed by the contractor for performance,

    2. The risk and responsibility assumed by the contractor for the costs of performance,

    3. The degree of oversight that must be exercised by the government over the contractor's performance,

    4. The degree and type of contract management that must be exercised by the contractor, and

    5. The amount and nature of the profit incentive offered to the contractor for achieving or exceeding specified standards or goals.

B. There are two basic families of contracts:

    1. Fixed price, where the performance and cost risks rest mainly with the contractor. (FAR 16.2/DFARS 216.2.)

    2. Cost reimbursement, where the performance and cost risks rest mainly with the government. (FAR 16.3/DFARS 216.3.)

II. Fixed-Price Contracts

A. Fixed-Price Contracts (FAR Subpart 16.2)

    1. Fixed-price contracts are the most common contract type and the closest to the typical commercial contract.

    2. Under a fixed-price contract, the contractor promises to perform at a fixed price and bears the responsibility for increased costs of performance. *ITT Arctic Servs., Inc. v. United States*, 207 Ct. Cl. 743 (1975); *Chevron U.S.A., Inc.*, ASBCA No. 32323, 90-1 BCA Par. 22,602 (the risk of increased performance costs in a fixed-price contract is on the contractor absent a clause stating otherwise). The contract price does not change unless the work required under the contract changes. The contractor is required to complete the contract whether or not the contractor incurs a loss on the contract price.

    3. The performance and cost risk to the government are smallest of any contract type, and the risks to the contractor are greatest. The contractor's incentive to assume these risks is the opportunity to earn additional profit if it can effectively control costs.

    4. For a fixed-price contract to be successful

        a. The government must draft clear specifications;

        b. The contractor must have a clear understanding of the work required, the acceptance criteria, and the costs that will be incurred to complete the work; and

        c. Both the contractor and the government must manage the contract so as to avoid "scope creep" (i.e., growth in contract requirements that will either require modification to the contract price or result in contract claims.)

B. Firm-Fixed-Price Contracts (FFP) (FAR 16.202)

1. An FFP contract provides for a price that is not subject to any adjustment on the basis of the contractor's cost experience on the contract. It places upon the contractor the maximum risk and full responsibility for all costs and resulting profit or loss, and thereby the maximum incentive to control costs and perform effectively. Compared to other contract types, it imposes a minimum administrative burden upon the contracting parties. (FAR 16.202-1.)

2. Use of an FFP contract is appropriate when acquiring commercial items or for acquiring other supplies or services on the basis of reasonably definite functional or detailed specifications when the contracting officer can establish fair and reasonable prices at the outset, such as when (FAR 16.202-2)

    a. There is adequate price competition;

    b. There are reasonable price comparisons with prior purchases of the same or similar supplies or services made on a competitive basis or supported by valid cost or pricing data;

    c. Available cost or pricing information permits realistic estimates of the probable costs of performance; or

    d. Performance uncertainties can be identified and reasonable estimates of their cost impact can be made, and the contractor is willing to accept a firm fixed price representing assumption of the risks involved.

3. Firm-fixed-price contracts can be awarded based on formally advertised or sealed-bid procurements, or can be negotiated based on cost and pricing data. If an award is made before the price is negotiated, the government awards a letter contract, as will be discussed later.

4. Use of an FFP contract is normally not appropriate for research and development work, and has been limited by DOD appropriations acts. See FAR 35.006(c) (the use of cost-reimbursement contracts is usually appropriate for R&D contracts); But see *AT&T v. United States*, 177 F.3d 1368 (Fed. Cir. 1999) (upholding a fixed-price contract for a developmental contract despite stated prohibition contained in FY 1987 Appropriations Act).

5. Some agencies require service contracts to be performance-based and fixed price.

6. A firm-fixed-price contract, which best utilizes the basic profit motive of a business enterprise, is to be used when the risk involved is minimal or can be

predicted with an acceptable degree of certainty. (FAR 16.103(b)). When a reasonable basis for firm pricing does not exist, however, other contract types should be considered, and negotiations should be directed toward selecting a contract type (or a combination of contract types) that will appropriately tie profit to contractor performance.

C. Fixed-Price Contracts with Economic Price Adjustment (FP-EPA) (FAR 16.203)

1. Fixed-price contracts with economic price adjustment are similar to firm-fixed-price contracts, but provide for upward and downward adjustments to the stated contract price upon the occurrence of specified contingencies. Price adjustments are typically tied to changes in material costs or labor rates, or both.

2. This type of contract should be used only when the contracting officer determines that it is necessary to protect the parties against significant fluctuations in labor or material costs, or to provide for contract price adjustment in the event of changes in the contractor's established prices. The assumption is that the conditions are such that they are beyond either party's ability to control or forecast.

3. The *FAR* describes three general types of contingencies that can be included in a contract and on which these adjustments can be made. (FAR 16.203-1.)

a. Adjustments may be based on an agreed-upon level in published or otherwise established prices of specific items or the contract end items. See FAR 52.216-2 (standard supplies) and FAR 52.216-3 (semistandard supplies); DFARS 216.203-4.

b. Adjustments may be based on actual increases or decreases in the cost of labor or material that the contractor experiences during contract performance. Variation in the specified costs must have at least a three percent impact on the contract price before any adjustment is required. (FAR 52.216.4(c)(3).) There is a maximum aggregate upward adjustment of 10 percent of the contract price. (FAR 52.216-4(c)(4).)

c. Adjustments may also be based on increases or decreases in the national cost indexes for labor or materials. The standards or indices are specifically identified in the contract. There is no standard *FAR* clause prescribed when using this method. However, various agency *FAR* supplements provide guidance. For example, the *DFARS* provides extensive guidelines for use of indexes. Similarly, the Air Force recognizes the abnormal escalation index method and the constant dollar index method.

d. If the agency drafts its own economic price adjustment (EPA) clauses, the clauses must be written to provide the contractor with the protection envisioned by regulation. Courts and boards will reform EPA clauses to conform with regulations. *Beta Systems. Inc. v. United States*, 838 F.2d 1179 (Fed. Cir. 1988) (reformation appropriate where chosen index failed to achieve purpose of EPA clause); *Craft Mach. Works. Inc.*, ASBCA No. 35167, 90-3 BCA Par. 23,095 (EPA clause did not provide contractor with inflationary adjustment from a base period paralleling the beginning of the contract, as contemplated by regulations).

    e. More than one cost ceiling may be used. *Commercial Energies. Inc.*, B-243616, Aug. 15, 1991, 91-2 CPD Par. 152 (agency could use two ceilings in contract for natural gas because the ceilings protected the government against two contingencies).

4. There are problems with the *FAR* EPA clauses:

    a. Lack of clarity as to economic factors to be considered,

    b. Ceiling/floor is 10 percent unless otherwise agreed,

    c. Timing of the adjustment,

    d. The effect of government/contractor changes and delays, and

    e. Contractor notice requirements and their impact on the right to an adjustment.

5. A contractor may waive its entitlement to an adjustment if it fails to submit its request within the time specified in the contract. *Bataco Indus.*, 29 Fed. Cl. 318 (1993) (contractor filed requests more than one year after EPA clause deadlines).

6. The contractor retains some risks and incentives:

    a. EPA clauses contain caps and ceilings, and

    b. The contractor will realize profits from other kinds of cost savings within its control.

7. Under DFARS 216.203-4, EPA clauses may be used only when the contract price is above the simplified acquisition threshold and the performance period is more than six months.

D. Fixed-Price Redeterminable Contracts (FP-R) (FAR 16.205 and 16.206)

1. Price redetermination is one-way—downward.

2. There are two types of fixed-price redeterminable contracts: prospective and retroactive.

a. Prospective. Price is fixed for initial quantities, but is adjusted periodically for future quantities based upon the contractor's cost experience. This type is useful on initial quantity production contracts (e.g., spare parts), where subsequent pricing periods are at least 12 months.

b. Retroactive. Price for work already performed is subject to redetermination based upon the contractor's actual cost experience. This type is used for R&D contracts with an estimated cost of $100,000 or less, where the contractor's accounting system is adequate for price redetermination, there is reasonable assurance that the redetermination will take place promptly at the specified time, and the head of contract activity approves its use in writing.

3. Redeterminable contracts have been rarely used since the 1970s because they are administratively burdensome and the contractor has little incentive to control costs.

E. Fixed-price incentive and award fee contracts, and fixed-price level of effort contracts, are discussed in Units 4 and 5.

III. Cost–Reimbursement Contracts

A. Introduction (FAR Subpart 16.3)

1. Cost-reimbursement contracts should be used when the costs of performance cannot be predicted with an acceptable level of accuracy. This may occur when the performance risk is high (e.g., cutting-edge technology, unproven design) and the scope of work is vague and ill-defined, and when there is no cost history on which to base cost and price estimates. Typically, research and development contracts are awarded on a cost-reimbursement basis.

2. The contractor only agrees to provide its "best efforts." Even if this results in no deliveries, the contractor is held harmless. If incurred costs are less than estimated, the "excess" (i.e., unspent) money is kept by the government. Conversely, any cost "overrun" (i.e., cost incurred in excess of the estimate) is paid by the government. Thus, the performance and cost risk to the contractor is small, and to the government is large.

3. The contractor's incentive is the ability to achieve a higher margin by completing work at lower costs, or by meeting or exceeding objective performance criteria.

4. Cost-reimbursement contracts provide for payment of allowable incurred costs plus a fee (often erroneously called profit) to the extent prescribed in the contract, and establish an estimate of total cost for the purpose of obligating funds.

5. To be allowable, a cost must be reasonable, allocable, properly accounted for, and not

specifically disallowed by the contract or by *FAR* cost principles. (FAR 31.201-2.) See Unit 3 for a more detailed discussion of cost allowability.

6. The contract establishes a cost ceiling that the contractor may not exceed (except at its own risk) without the contracting officer's approval. The contractor is not required to spend more money than the amount obligated under the contract. When the cost or funding ceiling, whichever is lower, is reached, the contractor can simply stop working even though the work is not technically completed.

7. The decision to use a cost-type contract is within the contracting officer's discretion. *Crimson Enters.*, B-243193, June 10, 1991, 91-1 CPD Par. 557 (decision to use cost-type contract reasonable considering uncertainty over requirements causing multiple changes); *Delco Elec. Corp.*, B-244559, Oct. 29, 1991, 91-2 CPD Par. 391 (selection of type committed to agency discretion and selection of firm-fixed-price found reasonable).

B. Limitations on Use of Cost-Type Contracts (FAR 16.301-3)

1. The contractor must have an adequate cost accounting system. See *CrystaComm, Inc.*, ASBCA No. 37177, 90-2 BCA Par. 22,692 (contractor failed to establish required cost accounting system).

2. The government must exercise appropriate surveillance to ensure the use of efficient methods and effective cost controls. The government will review and approve billed costs and may disallow "unapproved" costs.

3. The government pays on a provisional basis until the books are closed at the end of contract. At that time it may retroactively disallow costs. This can result in protracted contract closeouts.

4. As will be discussed further, there are statutory limits on allowable fees.

5. Cost-reimbursement contracts may not be used for acquisition of commercial items under FAR Part 12.

C. Cost Ceilings. A contractor performing on a cost-reimbursement contract does not have to spend money beyond the funding or cost ceiling. The government does not have to provide additional funding above the cost ceiling. Under the Anti-Deficiency Act, a government contracting officer cannot commit the government to spend more than has been allotted. Cost ceilings are imposed through the Limitation of Cost clause for fully funded contracts (FAR 52.232-20), or the Limitation of Funds clause for incrementally funded contracts (FAR 52.232-22).

1. The contractor must give the contracting officer advance notice of potential cost overruns. The contract clause requires the contractor to give advance notice when it

anticipates that within the next 30-90 days its actual costs will reach 75-85 percent of the fund or cost ceiling. The contractor should base this projection on a current estimate at completion (EAC) using its best available indirect rates.

2. FAR 32.704 provides that a contracting officer must, upon receipt of notice from the contractor, promptly obtain funding and programming information pertinent to the contract and inform the contractor in writing that either

    a. Additional funds have been allotted, or the estimated cost has been increased, in a specified amount;

    b. The contract is not to be funded further and the contractor should submit a proposal for the adjustment of fee, if any (based on the percentage of work completed in relation to the total work prescribed under the contract);

    c. The contract is to be terminated; or

    d. The government is considering whether to allot additional funds or increase the estimated cost, that the contractor is entitled to stop work when the funding or cost limit is reached, and that any work beyond the funding or cost limit will be at the contractor's risk. In such event, if the contracting officer learns that the contract will receive no further

funds, he or she must promptly give the contractor written notice of the decision not to provide funds.

3. The contractor may not recover costs above the ceiling unless the contracting officer authorizes the contractor to exceed the ceiling. *Titan Corp. v. West*, 129 F.3d 1479 (Fed. Cir. 1997); *SMS Agoura System, Inc.*, ASBCA No. 50451, 97-2 BCA Par. 29,203. If the contractor continues to incur costs above the ceiling or otherwise fails to provide required notice, it will be performing "at risk." This highlights the need for contractors to have adequate accounting and management information systems.

4. The contracting officer may issue a change order, a direction to replace or repair defective items or work, or a termination notice, without immediately increasing the funds available. Since a contractor is not obligated to incur costs in excess of the estimated cost in the contract, the contracting officer may direct that any increase in the estimated cost or amount allotted to a contract be used for the sole purpose of funding termination or other specified expenses.

5. There are exceptions to this "no recovery above the ceiling" rule:

    a. The overrun was unforeseeable. *RMI. Inc. v. United States*, 800 F.2d 246 (Fed. Cir. 1986); or

b. The government induced the contractor to continue working even though funding was not available. *American Elec. Labs., Inc. v. United States*, 774 F.2d 1110 (Fed. Cir. 1985) (successfully asserted); *Southwest Marine of San Francisco. Inc.* ASBCA No. 33404, 89-1 BCA Par. 21,425 (unsuccessfully asserted).

D. Cost-Plus-Fixed-Fee (CPFF) Contracts (FAR 16.306)

1. The contract price is the contractor's allowable costs, plus a fixed fee, which is negotiated and set prior to award. The fee is calculated (in advance) as a percentage of the estimated cost proposed under the contract, rather than the percentage of costs actually incurred. This may result in a different "margin" (but not a different fee) if actual costs differ from estimated costs.

    a. For example, suppose the parties agree to a fixed fee of $10,000 for a contract whose estimated costs are $100,000. The estimated contract price will then be $110,000 ($100,000 + $10,000), with an estimated margin of 9.09 percent ($10,000 / $110,000).

    b. If in fact the actual costs incurred by the contractor are $200,000, the contractor will still get a fixed fee of $10,000, making the actual contract price $210,000 ($200,000 + $10,000), with an actual margin of 4.76 percent ($10,000 / $210,000).

2. The fee should include profit, plus an amount for unallowable costs. It may be adjusted only if contract requirements change.

3. Limitation on maximum fee. CPFF contracts are subject to specific limitations on the percentage of fee that can be paid to the contractor. See 10 U.S.C. § 2306(d); 41 U.S.C. § 254(b); FAR 15.404-4(c)(4).

    a. Maximum fee limitations are based on the estimated cost at the time of award, not on the actual costs incurred.

    b. For research and development contracts, the maximum fee is a specific amount no greater than 15 percent of the estimated cost at the time of award.

    c. For architect/engineer (A/E) contracts for public works and utilities, the maximum fee is six percent of the estimated cost of construction.

    d. For contracts other than R&D and A/E contracts, the maximum fee is a specific amount no greater than 10 percent of the estimated cost at the time of award.

4. The fixed fee may be a loss. See *Lockheed-Georgia Co.. Div. of Lockheed Corp.*, ASBCA No. 27660, 90-3 BCA Par. 22,957 (FPI contract converted to fixed loss for initial C-5A production contract).

5. By law (e.g., Military Construction Appropriations Act, 2002. P.L. 107-6, §101), DOD agencies may not use CPFF contracts on construction contracts estimated to exceed $25,000 that are funded by a military construction appropriations act, and are to be performed in the United States (except Alaska). (DFARS 216.306.)

E. Cost-Reimbursement (CR) Contracts (FAR 16.302)

1. Under a straight cost reimbursement contract, a contractor is reimbursed only for allowable costs actually incurred to perform the contract. The contractor is not usually paid a fee or profit and is not required to incur costs in excess of the amount funded.

2. This type of contract is most commonly used for research and development work, particularly for nonprofit and educational organizations. Although a fee is usually not awarded under a contract to a nonprofit organization, a management fee is sometimes allowed to compensate the nonprofit organization for some nonrecoverable or unallowable costs.

3. A cost-reimbursement contract may also be used for a facilities contract.

F. Cost-Sharing Contracts (FAR 16.303)

1. In a cost-sharing contract, the contractor is reimbursed for only an agreed-upon portion of its allowable cost.

2. This kind of contract is normally used where the contractor will receive substantial benefit from the effort (e.g., in research and development contracts), or where the purpose of the contract is use in marketing opportunities in the commercial marketplace.

G. No-Cost Contracts

1. Under a no-cost contract, the contractor agrees to provide something (typically, services) with no financial obligation on the part of the government.

2. The contractor hopes to recoup its costs and make a profit by charging a third party, such as the general public, for the deliverables or services. For example, the contractor might provide stenographic reporting services at federal agency hearings at no charge to the government, but be compensated by charging interested parties for transcripts.

3. The contractor must receive some kind of nonmonetary consideration (e.g., exclusive access or rights) in order for the contract to be binding and enforceable.

H. Cost-reimbursement incentive and award-fee contracts are discussed in Unit 4.

UNIT 03

Applicable Accounting Regulations

Contract Types

I. Why do we need to understand what things cost?

A. Cost accounting can determine how much a contractor will be paid.

B. Cost accounting may affect a contractor's decisions. Inaccurate or unreliable cost information may lead to bad business decisions concerning

   1. Estimating and pricing;

   2. Allocation of resources, staffing, and investments; and

   3. Strategic priorities.

C. Although cost accounting is most relevant to cost-reimbursement contracts, proper cost accounting is necessary for all types of contracts.

   1. Cost accounting is needed for the pricing of contracts, subcontracts, and modifications to contracts and subcontracts whenever cost analysis (FAR 15.404-1(c)) is performed.

   2. In all contracts, it is important for the contractor to have proper information for cost estimating, billing, and revenue recognition purposes.

   3. In cost-reimbursement contracts, it is necessary for the contractor to have proper cost accounting to be able to invoice properly and to satisfy limitation of cost/limitation of funds requirements.

   In a cost-reimbursement contract, a contractor will be paid only its verified (and allowable) costs. Inaccurate or unverifiable cost information may result in unreimbursed costs.

   4. Even in fixed-price contracts, proper cost accounting may be necessary to support progress payment billings, equitable adjustments for contract changes, and claims under the Contract Disputes Act.

   5. Reliable cost accounting systems are needed to calculate estimates to complete (ETC)/estimates at completion (EAC), earned value management system (EVMS) reports, and cost accounting standards (CAS) accounting change impact statements.

   6. Cost accounting is needed to support termination settlement proposals under FAR Part 49.

D. Charging for unallowable costs may lead to civil and even criminal sanctions.

E. Government cost accounting rules are not generally used outside the federal government marketplace, since commercial companies do not generally charge customers on the basis of their costs. Therefore, commercial companies do not have to follow government accounting rules and are free to do their accounting in a way that helps their management processes. For example,

   1. They can account for cost by product or product line,

2. They do not have to do full absorption accounting, and

3. Their allocation of home office costs to business segments can be inconsistent.

F. Government cost accounting rules can be found in Title 48 of the Code of Federal Regulations:

1. Chapter 1: *Federal Acquisition Regulation (FAR)*, Part 31—Cost Principles—Cost Allowability.

2. Chapters 2–98: *FAR* Supplements.

3. Chapter 99: Cost Accounting Standards.

II. *FAR* COST ACCOUNTING PRINCIPLES (FAR PART 31)

A. Cost allowability (FAR 31.201-2). A cost is "allowable" only when it is

1. Reasonable;

2. Allocable;

3. Consistent with the cost accounting standards (CAS), if applicable, or generally accepted accounting principles (GAAP) otherwise;

4. Consistent with the terms of the contract; and

5. Consistent with the limitations in FAR 31.205.

B. A cost is "reasonable" if it does not exceed the amount that "would be incurred by a prudent business person in the conduct of a competitive business." (FAR 31.201-3)

1. The *FAR* identifies several considerations in making the "reasonableness" determination:

a. Is the cost recognized as "ordinary and necessary"?

b. Does the cost demonstrate accepted sound business practices, arm's length bargaining, and compliance with federal and state laws and regulations?

c. Is the cost consistent with the contractor's responsibilities to customers, owners, and employees?

d. Does the cost conform to the contractor's established practices?

2. There is no presumption of reasonableness—that is, there is no presumption that if the cost was incurred in an arm's length transaction it must have been reasonable. If there is a question about the reasonableness of a cost, the burden of proof will be on the contractor.

C. A cost is "allocable" (FAR 31.201-4) if it

1. Is incurred specifically for the contract;

2. Benefits both the contract and other work, distributed in a reasonable proportion to the benefits received; or

3. Is necessary to the overall operation of the business, even without a direct relationship to any particular contract or cost objective.

D. Direct costs are related to a particular cost objective and can be traced to it in an economically feasible way. A *cost objective* is typically a specific contract or a specific task order. Examples of direct costs would be direct labor cost (i.e., salaries) of those working specifically on the contract, the cost of materials used specifically for the contract, subcontractor costs, and "other direct costs." (FAR 31.202.)

E. Indirect costs are costs that are identified with two or more final cost objectives or intermediate cost objectives. They are usually grouped into common pools and charged to the contracts or cost objectives that benefit by means of an allocation or indirect cost rate, using the following process (FAR 31.203):

1. Cost objectives are identified. These may be "final" or "intermediate," and are typically a contract, task order, or project (such as R&D or bid and proposal (B&P)).

2. Indirect costs are captured into logical groupings, which are called "pools."

3. An appropriate cost allocation base is selected for each indirect cost pool. It should have a relation to the benefit received from the indirect costs incurred.

4. The indirect rate (per unit of the cost allocation base) is calculated for each pool.

   a. This indirect rate determines the amount of indirect costs that will be allocated to each contract (or cost objective).

   b. The indirect rate is calculated by dividing the aggregate indirect costs collected in the pool by the cost allocation base.

   c. For example, if the contractor has established an indirect cost pool consisting of all fringe benefit costs and has chosen to allocate this pool over direct labor costs, the indirect rate would be:

   Indirect Cost Rate = Indirect Cost Pool (e.g., all fringe benefit costs) / Cost Base (e.g., all direct labor costs).

5. Costs are assigned to the cost objectives by multiplying the indirect rate by the applicable part of the cost allocation base. For example, in the previous system, the contract allocation would be

   Allocation to contract = Indirect Cost Rate x Direct Labor Costs on Contract

F. Typical indirect cost pools and rates include

1. Fringe benefits cost pool (vacation, sick leave, holiday, health insurance, pension, FICA, etc.), which is normally allocated using all direct labor dollars as the allocation base;

2. Overhead cost pool (supplies, office space, supervisory and support labor), which is normally allocated using direct labor dollars as the allocation base;

3. General and administrative (G&A) cost pool (management, legal, human resources, home office), which is normally allocated using a total cost input allocation base (i.e., all contract costs, not just direct labor costs).

G. During the contracting cycle, indirect cost rates may evolve:

1. Forward pricing rates are used for cost estimates. They should reflect the best estimate of indirect cost rates expected during the upcoming accounting period. The contractor may negotiate a separate forward pricing rate agreement with the ACO, covering the indirect rates to be used for estimating indirect costs for future government contract work (FAR 42.1701).

2. Provisional billing rates may be used for *interim* billings of costs (FAR 42.704). These should be revised during the year as necessary, based on mutual agreement, and should be updated soon after year-end.

3. An internal booking rate—for example, percentage of completion—may be used by the contractor for revenue recognition purposes. This rate may or may not be the same as the provisional billing rate; it is not used for billing purposes and is not subject to audit by the government.

4. A proposed final indirect cost rate proposal must be submitted within six months after the contractor's fiscal year ends. It will be audited by DCAA. In the event the contractor's submission is late, the government may establish final indirect rates unilaterally.

5. Final indirect cost rates are rates that have been audited and settled with the government and are used for billing adjustments (if they are different from provisional rates) and contract closeout (final payments).

6. Quick closeout rates are used for quick closeout purposes when settlement of final rates is delayed. These rates are final for the covered contract, but will not serve as a precedent for the rates to be used for other contracts. (FAR 42.708.) The quick closeout procedure may be used if

   a. The contract is physically complete;

   b. The amount of unsettled indirect cost to be allocated to the contract is relatively insignificant. (Under the *FAR*, the amount of unsettled indirect costs is "insignificant" if it does not exceed $1,000,000 on any one contract and, cumulatively, 15 percent of the total indirect costs allocable to cost-type contracts. This restriction may be waived by the contracting officer based on a risk assessment.)

 c. Agreement can be reached on a reasonable estimate of allocable dollars.

7. Advance Agreements. It may be advisable or even necessary to enter into an advance agreement with the government concerning the treatment of a specific cost under a particular contract. (FAR 31.109.)

H. Limitations in FAR 31.205

1. FAR 31.205 contains rules covering more than 50 specific cost items. Certain costs are considered unallowable for reasons of public policy, such as the costs of alcoholic beverages (FAR 31.205-51). Other costs are subject to restrictions in kind or amount, such as lobbying expenses (FAR 31.205-22). And many of the cost principles provide clarity and definition to specific allowable costs.

2. In addition to the cost principles expressed in FAR 31.205, many agencies have supplemental cost principles. To fully assess a cost allowability issue, a contractor should review not only the *FAR* cost principles but also any specific agency supplemental cost principles.

3. Changes often occur in the cost principles, making the effective date of a particular change important. Generally, the cost principles applied to a contract are those that were in effect as of the date of contract award. When a cost issue is not directly addressed in section 31.205, however, a later regulation dealing with that cost treatment may become critical in determining whether the costs were allowable in prior periods.

4. The applicability date can affect the timing of a cost disallowance. Cost allowability issues often arise after the costs have been incurred. Meanwhile, the contractor is structuring its bids and proposals and budgeting overhead rates based on prior cost figures. A retroactive disallowance may affect not only past costs, but also future budgeted costs. To minimize these risks, it is important that contractors do everything possible to submit their historical overhead rates quickly and close out contracts as early as possible.

I. Unallowable Costs

1. Unallowable costs must be identified and excluded from billings, claims, and proposals. These include costs that do not meet the reasonableness test, costs that do not meet allocability requirements, costs that are specifically excluded by the contract, and costs that do not satisfy the FAR 31.205 restrictions.

2. Per FAR 52.242-4, contracts above $650,000 that require the submission of final indirect cost rates also require submission of a certification of final indirect costs. An individual at the level of vice president or chief financial officer in the business segment submitting the indirect rate proposal must certify that they have reviewed the proposal and that to the best of their knowledge and belief,

   a. All costs included in the proposal are allowable in accordance with the applicable *FAR* cost principles; and

   b. The proposal does not include any costs that are expressly unallowable under applicable *FAR* cost principles.

3. If unallowable costs are included in an indirect rate submission, the penalty may include the amount of expressly unallowable costs allocated to covered contracts, or double that amount if the inclusion was with the contractor's knowledge, and interest. (FAR 42.709-1.) These penalties can be reduced or waived if the contractor withdraws its Final Rate Proposal before an audit begins, or if the amount is under $10,000 or the inclusion of unallowable costs was inadvertent.

J. Contract Financing and Milestone Billings

1. Financing and interim payment issues are not unique to government contracts; they arise in commercial contracts as well.

2. Normally, the contractor delivers the product or service identified in the contract, submits an invoice for payment, and is paid.

3. Milestone billings allow payments before final delivery. They coincide with identified (and tangible) events during contract performance that are performance-related, schedule-related, or called out by a separate contract line item number (CLIN).

4. The government may provide contract "financing" in order to maintain a broad base of suppliers. Many government contracts are long-term contracts, and companies need financing in order to be able to perform. Absent financing, many contractors would leave the marketplace, and a broad base of suppliers is in the government's interest because it enhances competition and provides expansion capability in times of emergency. In addition, contract financing availability is essential to the government's small business policy objectives. Among the forms of contract financing are

   a. Advance payments (loans)—FAR 52.232-12;

   b. Cost reimbursements for cost-reimbursement contracts (excluding services)—FAR 52.216-7;

   c. Progress payments for fixed-price contracts (80 percent of incurred cost)—FAR 52.232-16; and

d. Performance-based payments for fixed-price contracts—FAR 52.232-32.

5. Contractors can improve cash flow in various ways, such as by

   a. Analyzing billing rates and proposed adjustments as soon as possible after year-end;

   b. Requesting release of fee retainage when final indirect rates are submitted. FAR 52.216-8 provides that contracting officers shall release between 75 and 90 percent of fee withholds for otherwise completed contracts; and

   c. Looking for quick closeout opportunities.

K. The Prompt Payment Act generally requires that the government must pay the contractor within 30 days of receipt of a "proper invoice" (unless the contract provides otherwise).

   1. Requests for interim financing are not considered invoices.

   2. If payment is not made within 15 days of the due date the government must pay interest, calculated as simple interest using the Treasury Renegotiation Rate.

III. Cost Accounting Standards (48 C.F.R. Part 9904; FAR Part 30)

A. The Cost Accounting Standards (CAS) are a group of accounting rules that dictate how the costs of government contractors must be measured, accumulated, assigned to years, and allocated to contracts.

   1. As originally promulgated in the 1970s, the CAS applied only to negotiated DOD contracts. In 1998, the CAS was extended to apply to negotiated civilian agency contracts.

   2. The CAS concern allocation, as opposed to allowability of costs. See, generally, *Westinghouse Elec. Corp.*, ASBCA No. 25685, 82-2 BCA Par. 15,960.

   3. The CAS requirements are codified at Title 48, Chapter 99 of the Code of Federal Regulations. Further CAS guidance can be found in FAR Part 30 and DFARS Part 230.

B. The Cost Accounting Standards apply

   1. To negotiated contracts and subcontracts (FAR Part 15) in excess of $650,000;

   2. If the contractor is currently performing a $7.5 million "trigger" contract.

C. CAS-covered contracts may be subject to either "full" or "modified" CAS coverage.

   1. A contractor will be subject to full CAS coverage (i.e., all 19 CAS standards will apply) if its business unit receives (48 C.F.R. 9903.201-2(a))

      a. A single CAS-covered contract of $50 million or more, or

b. $50 million or more in "net CAS-covered awards" (which includes the potential value of contract options) during its preceding cost accounting period.

2. A contractor subject to "modified" CAS coverage may be required to file a disclosure statement (to be discussed further) and is required to comply with the following four standards:

a. CAS 401—Consistency in Estimating, Accumulating, and Reporting Costs,

b. CAS 402—Consistency in Allocating Costs Incurred for the Same Purpose,

c. CAS 405—Accounting for Unallowable Costs, and

d. CAS 406—Cost Accounting Period.

C. The following contracts are exempt from CAS requirements (48 C.F.R. 9903.201-1(b)):

1. Sealed bid contracts (under FAR Part 14);

2. Negotiated contracts and subcontracts below $650,000;

3. Contracts and subcontracts with small businesses;

4. Contracts with prices set by law or regulation;

5. Commercial item contracts (firm fixed price, fixed price with economic price

adjustment, time and materials, and labor hour) under FAR Part 12;

6. Contractors who do not have any CAS-covered contracts of $7.5 million or more;

7. Contracts performed entirely outside the United States; and

8. Firm-fixed-price contracts with adequate price competition and without submissions of cost or pricing data.

E. Certain contractors and subcontractors are required by statute to disclose in writing and comply with their cost accounting practices (41 U.S.C. § 422). A contractor must submit a CAS disclosure statement (48 C.F.R. § 9903.202-1(b)) if it receives a single award of $50 million or more, or if it was awarded CAS-covered contracts totaling $50 million or more in the preceding cost accounting period.

1. A business segment will be exempt if its CAS-covered awards were below $10 million and less than 30 percent of total company sales.

2. After its disclosure statement has been approved, a contractor must notify the ACO before implementing any accounting changes. If those changes might change the amount allocated to cost-reimbursement contracts, it must file a CAS impact statement and may be required to provide consideration to the government for any increases in cost recoveries, (but it will not,

of course, receive consideration for decreases in cost recovery!)

F. The disclosure statement must be filed

1. If based on prior year awards, at the award of the first CAS-covered contract or within 90 days of the start of the next fiscal year; or

2. If based on a single award, prior to award.

G. The format for a disclosure statement is as follows:

1. Part 1—General information

2. Part 2—Direct Costs

3. Part 3—Direct vs. Indirect Costs

4. Part 4—Indirect Costs

5. Part 5—Depreciation and Capitalization

6. Part 6—Other Costs and Credits

7. Part 7—Deferred Compensation and Insurance

8. Part 8—Corporate or Group Expenses

9. Continuation Sheets

H. CAS Concepts and Rules that are referenced in the *FAR*:

1. CAS 402: Consistency in Allocating Costs Incurred for the Same Purpose

2. CAS 405: Accounting for Unallowable Costs

3. CAS 409: Depreciation of Tangible Capital Assets

4. CAS 412: Composition and Measurement of Pension Cost

5. CAS 413: Adjustment and Allocation of Pension Cost

6. CAS 414: Cost of Money as an Element of the Cost of Facilities Capital

7. CAS 415: Deferred Compensation

8. CAS 416: Accounting for Insurance Costs

9. CAS 417: Cost of Money as an Element of the Cost of Capital Assets under Construction

10. CAS 420: Accounting for IR&D and B&P Costs

I. CAS Allocation Standards:

1. CAS 403: Allocation of Home Office Expenses to Segments

2. CAS 410: Allocation of Business Unit G&A to Final Cost Objectives

3. CAS 418: Allocation of Direct & Indirect Costs

4. CAS 420: Accounting for IR&D/B&P Costs

J. Example—CAS 418: Allocation of Direct and Indirect Costs

1. The purpose of this standard is to provide:

   a. Consistent determination of direct and indirect costs,

   b. Criteria for the accumulation of indirect costs in pools, and

   c. Guidance for selecting allocation measures based on beneficial or causal relationships between an indirect cost pool and cost objectives.

2. CAS 418 requirements requires a written policy that

   a. Classifies costs as direct or indirect,

   b. Is consistently applied,

   c. Accumulates indirect costs in homogeneous pools, and

   d. Allocates pools to cost objectives in reasonable proportion to benefits received (by the cost objectives).

IV. The Truth in Negotiations Act

A. The Truth in Negotiations Act (10 U.S.C. 2306a and 41 U.S.C. 254b) is sometimes known as TINA.

1. TINA provides that when price is to be negotiated, the offeror must submit certified cost or pricing data. If the data is not current, not accurate, or not complete, the contract price shall be adjusted downward, as necessary.

2. The purpose of the act is to place the government and the contractor in an equal negotiating posture.

3. No intent to defectively price, or actual knowledge of defective data, is required for a TINA violation. Bad data is bad data.

B. Per FAR 2.101, cost or pricing data is information that satisfies the following requirements:

1. It is factual, not judgmental;

2. It is information that a prudent person would expect to have a significant effect on price;

3. It is verifiable; and

4. It is available through the date of the agreement on price.

C. Contracts are exempt from TINA requirements, and cost or pricing data should not be required, when (FAR 15.403-1)

1. The contracting officer determines that prices are based on adequate price competition;

25

2. The acquisition is below $650,000 (FAR 15.403-4(a)(1));

3. The price is set by law or regulation;

4. A commercial item is being acquired (FAR Part 12); or

5. A waiver is granted.

D. Even if a contract is exempt from TINA requirements, the contracting officer may request information *other* than cost or pricing data to determine that proposed prices are fair and reasonable (FAR 15.403-3). This may include prices at which the same or similar items have previously been sold, and other cost data. The contractor will not, however, be required to execute a certification.

E. Adequate price competition exists when

1. Two or more responsible offerors, competing independently, submit priced offers, *and*

   a. Price is a substantial factor in source selection, and

   b. The price is not found to be unreasonable. Or,

2. One offer is received, but there was a reasonable expectation *by that offeror* that two or more competitors would submit offers; or

3. A price analysis clearly demonstrates that the proposed price is reasonable in comparison with current or recent prices for the same or similar items (adjusted to reflect changes in market conditions and contract terms) under contracts that *did* result from adequate price competition.

F. A TINA violation may occur even if

1. The contractor does not intend to defectively price, or

2. The contractor's price negotiator does not have actual knowledge of the defective data.

3. The acid test is whether the information would affect, to any degree, the buyer's or seller's negotiating position. If so, the government will probably claim that the information is cost or pricing data.

G. TINA requires the contractor to file a certificate of current cost or pricing data (FAR 15.403-4(b)(2), 15.406-2).

1. The contractor must certify that it has disclosed accurate, complete, and current cost or pricing data.

2. The data must be accurate, current, and complete as of the date of price agreement, also know as the "handshake date."

3. The certificate of current cost or pricing data should be executed as soon as practicable after the handshake date.

4. Even if the contractor does not execute a certification, it is subject to the requirements of TINA; the failure to certify is not a defense to defective pricing allegations.

H. Failure to comply with Truth In Negotiations Act requirements can lead to (FAR 15.407-1, 52.215-10, -11, -12, -13)

   1. Price reductions, including cost, fee, interest on any overpayments, and penalties (FAR 15.407-1);

   2. An investigation, and possible prosecution, for fraud;

   3. Suspension or debarment; and

   4. Allegations of violations of other statutes (e.g., False Claims Act, False Statements Act, Conspiracy, Wire/Mail Fraud, etc.)

I. The targets (and potential defendants) of defective pricing audits are not just accountants. They include

   1. Upper management (e.g., undisclosed results of strategic planning, budgets, planned merger and acquisition (M&A) activity);

   2. Financial managers (e.g., budget/actual variance analysis);

   3. Buyers, subcontract managers, purchasing managers (e.g, undisclosed vendor

bids, negotiation history, or cost/price analyses);

   4. Engineers (e.g., undisclosed cost estimates, make or buy decisions);

   5. Contract negotiators and sales and marketing personnel;

   6. Industrial relations managers (e.g., planned changes to production flows);

J. Potential causes of defective pricing

   1. Supplier costs are not current (e.g., rebates).

   2. Rates are inaccurate (e.g., not monitored or updated).

   3. Labor estimate is inaccurate (e.g., technical solution has changed).

   4. Management decisions are not disclosed (e.g., reorganization, accounting change).

K. Contractors have only limited defenses to defective pricing charges.

   1. The missing data is not "cost or pricing data" (the burden of proof is on the contractor).

   2. The missing data was not reasonably available before agreement on price.

   3. The government had actual notice of the missing data.

27

4. The parties would not have relied on the missing data (the burden of proof is on the contractor).

5. Any price decrease should be set off against price increases that would be justified by other missing data (of which the contractor was unaware).

6. The contract is exempt from TINA.

UNIT 04

INCENTIVE-TYPE CONTRACTS

Contract Types

I. Introduction

A. Incentive contracts are used when contract risks are moderate and other types of fixed-price or cost-reimbursement contracts are not appropriate.

B. Incentive contracts impose some risks on contractors without requiring full assumption of risks. They incentivize contractors to economize on costs, perform more efficiently, and/or adopt innovative performance/management techniques.

   1. The contractor realizes higher profits/fees by completing the work below a ceiling price or by meeting or exceeding objective performance targets.

   2. The government benefits by obtaining an end item or service at a lower cost, with greater performance, or ahead of schedule.

C. Incentive contracts may be either fixed price or cost reimbursement. The main difference is the contractor's obligation to deliver (in a fixed-price contract). The fee is determined either by a formula or by a process that includes a minimum fee, an incentive fee (based on performance), and a maximum fee.

D. Incentives may be objective or subjective.

   1. **Objective**: The parties include a formula in the contract to determine the amount of profit to be earned based on actual performance results achieved. The contract can be either cost plus incentive fee (CPIF) or fixed price incentive (FPI).

   2. **Subjective**: The parties agree that the profit earned will be determined by the government based on its appraisal of the contractor's performance. The contract can be either cost plus award fee (CPAF) or fixed price award fee (FPAF).

E. Incentive fee contracts encourage cost, schedule, or performance improvement, based on quantifiable, measurable criteria.

   1. Cost criteria—using a share ratio for cost savings stated in government/contractor percentages (e.g., 60/40).

   2. Schedule criteria (e.g., early delivery of acceptable product).

   3. Performance criteria—must be measurable (e.g., payload, accuracy, etc.).

II. Incentive Fee Contracts

A. Cost-Plus-Incentive-Fee (CPIF) Contracts (FAR 16.304, FAR 16.405-1)

   1. Under a CPIF contract, a contractor is reimbursed for the actual costs incurred to perform the contract. To provide an incentive for the contractor to control costs during contract performance, the government awards a fee based on the contractor's performance as measured against a target. The target is usually the contractor's cost estimate as proposed and awarded. The incentive fee is a range of percentages based on whether the contractor's actual costs are below or above the cost estimate.

2. The CPIF specifies a target cost, a target fee, minimum and maximum fees, and a fee adjustment formula (share ratio). After contract performance, the fee is adjusted in accordance with the formula.

3. The target fee is reduced if actual incurred costs exceed the target cost, but not below a stated minimum. Setting fee percentages based on the original cost estimate avoids the prohibition on cost-plus-percentage-of-cost (CPPC) contracting. The actual fee, as adjusted, will not exceed a specified ceiling or fall below a specified floor.

4. If the contractor overruns its estimated cost under a CPIF contract, it will be reimbursed for the excess cost (funds permitting).

5. A CPIF is appropriate for services or development and test programs.

6. The government may combine technical incentives with cost incentives. (FAR 16.405-1(b)(2))

B. Fixed-Price-Incentive (FPI) Contracts (FAR 16.204; 16.403)

1. An FPI contract provides for adjusting profit and establishing the final contract price by application of a formula based on the relationship of the total final negotiated cost to the total target cost. The final price is subject to a price ceiling that is negotiated at the outset of the contract.

2. The contractor must complete a specified amount of work for a fixed price.

3. Profit is adjusted for superior cost performance, but the target cost is fixed. So, unlike a CPIF contract, if a contractor overruns (or underruns) the cost estimate in an FPI contract, the contractor will not be reimbursed or required to pay back the difference.

4. A target cost, target profit, ceiling price, profit range, and profit formula (share ratio) are established in the contract. Upon completion of the contract, costs are negotiated to determine the profit to be awarded. Costs in excess of the target cost reduce the profit according to the established contract formula. Costs below the target increase the profit. However, the price ceiling caps the contractor's total payments under the contract. The contractor bears all costs above the ceiling price.

5. There is a point of total absorption (PTA) at which the government's cost share equals the difference between the ceiling price and the target price. Above this point, the contractor "eats" all remaining cost—in effect, the share ratio becomes 100/0.

6. The government also benefits by using the resulting historical cost figures to negotiate future contracts for additional items or spare parts. This is important for contracts that do not include spares in the system contract.

7. Individual line items may have separate incentive provisions.

8. Use the FPI contract only when an FFP contract is not suitable but the parties can predict the cost of performance with a reasonable degree of accuracy.

9. The parties may use either FPI–firm target or FPI–successive targets.

   a. FPI–firm target specifies a target cost, a target profit, a price ceiling, and a profit adjustment formula.

   b. FPI–successive targets specifies an initial target cost, an initial target profit, an initial profit adjustment formula, the production point (typically at 20 percent of performance) at which the firm target cost and profit will be negotiated, and a ceiling price.

III. Award Fee Contracts

A. Cost-Plus-Award-Fee (CPAF) Contracts (FAR 16.305 and 16.405-2)

1. Under a CPAF contract, the contractor receives its costs, plus a fee consisting of a base fee (which may be as low as zero) and an award amount based upon the government's assessment of the contractor's performance. An award fee contract is appropriate when the government wants to provide an incentive for contract performance and wants that incentive to be based on technical criteria as well as cost control. Increasing contract complexity creates problems with formulas and gravitates toward award fee–type contracts.

2. Although a CPAF contract usually bases the award fee on technical performance considerations, FAR 16.402-1(a) provides that no incentive contract may provide for other incentives without also providing a cost incentive.

3. An award fee plan is established, which sets forth the amount of award fee that will be available (the award-fee pool), the award fee periods, and the criteria under which the award fee will be awarded. The plan may or may not allow unawarded portions of the award-fee pool to "roll over" into future period pools. Where possible, the contractor should attempt to provide input into the plan before it is finalized.

4. Limitations on Base Fee: Many agencies impose limits on the amount of base fee that an agency can agree to pay. For example, DOD contracts limit base fees to three percent of the estimated cost of the contract, exclusive of fee. (DFARS 216.405-2(c)(ii))

5. A technical committee (performance evaluation board) is frequently established to determine how the contractor performed against the quality and delivery requirements established by the contract. The award

fee is determined unilaterally by this committee, or by the contracting officer or award fee determination official, and is not subject to the disputes clause. The contractor can, however, challenge a misapplication of the award fee plan (though not the government's subjective findings). *Burnside-Ott Aviation Training Center vs. Dalton*, 107 F. 3d 854 (Fed. Cir. 1997).

6. A contractor is entitled to unpaid award fee when the government terminates a cost-plus-award-fee contract for convenience. *Northrop Grumman Corp. v. Goldin*, 136 F.3d 1479 (Fed. Cir. 1998), reversing *Grumman Space Station Integration Div.*, ASBCA No. 48719, 97-1 BCA Par. 28,843.

7. A CPAF contract provides for evaluations at stated intervals during performance, so the contractor will periodically be informed of the quality of its performance and the areas in which improvement is expected. Partial payment shall generally correspond to the evaluation periods. (FAR 16.405-2(b)(3))

8. Because an award fee contract provides for periodic assessments, it can improve communication between the contractor and the government. The award fee process can be administratively burdensome, however, and may "chill" the contractor's willingness to "stand up for its rights" in an adversary process.

9. The award fee schedule determines when the award fee payments are made. The fee schedule does not need to be proportional to the work completed. *Textron Defense Sys. v. Widnall*, 143 F.3d 1465 (Fed. Cir. 1998) (end-loading award fee to later periods).

10. CFAF contracts were first used by NASA in the 1960s and continue to be used extensively by NASA. (CPAF contracts consist of 48 percent of all dollars and 7.7 percent of all contracts.) They are used less frequently by DOD (13 percent of all dollars and 3.4 percent of all contracts.)

B. Fixed-Price with Award Fee Contracts (FAR 16.404)

1. The contractor receives a negotiated fixed price (which includes normal profit) and an additional award fee based upon the quality of its performance.

2. The contract must provide for periodic evaluation of the contractor's performance against an award fee plan.

3. This type of contract should be used when the government wants to motivate a contractor and other incentives cannot be used because the contractor's performance cannot be measured objectively.

4. The following conditions must be present before a fixed-price contract with award fee may be used:

    a.   The administrative costs of conducting award fee evaluations are not expected to exceed the expected benefits;

    b.   Procedures have been established for conducting the award fee evaluation;

    c.   The award fee board has been established; and

    d.   An individual above the level of the contracting officer approved the fixed-price award fee incentive.

C.   Award Term Contracts

1.   An award term contract contains a performance incentive that ties the length of a contract's term to the performance of the contractor. The contract term can be extended for good performance or reduced for poor performance. Award term contracts were initiated by the Air Force in 1996.

2.   It is similar to an award fee contract in that performance assessments are made regularly during the life of a contract.

3.   Award term solicitations and contracts should include a base period (e.g., three years) and a maximum term (e.g., 10 years), similar to quantity estimates used in indefinite quantity/ indefinite delivery contracts for supplies. (See Unit 5).

4.   There are special challenges related to award term contracts:

    a.   Contractors assume greater risk when pricing long-term contracts.

    b.   The government must comply with the *FAR*'s five-year limitation on consulting service contracts.

    c.   The parties must consider the effect of the government's right to terminate for convenience.

    d.   The government must satisfy *FAR* requirements for full and open competition.

UNIT 05

Other Contract Types and Agreements

Contract Types

I. Level-of-Effort Contracts (Time and Materials, Labor Hour) (FAR 16.6)

Unlike the typical completion contract, the contractor need not accomplish a specific task to complete a level-of-effort contract. It need only devote a specific amount of labor toward the task. The contract usually specifies the type of labor or professional skill required and an estimate of the number of hours of each job code.

A. Firm-Fixed-Price (FFP)/Level-of-Effort (LOE) Contracts (FAR 15.207)

    1. An FFP/LOE contract is much like a regular FFP contract, but with one major difference—the level-of-effort requirement. Under the level-of-effort clause, a contractor is required to incur a specified number of labor hours in categories of labor applicable to key personnel, to be performed in a specific period of time. Payment is based upon effort, not results. If the contractor incurs fewer hours, the contract price is adjusted downward according to a specified formula.

    2. An FFP/LOE contract is usually proposed for a fixed-price research and development–type contract. The deliverable is typically a report showing the results achieved through application of the required level of effort.

    3. Per FAR 16.207-3, an FFP/LOE contract may only be used when

        a. The work required cannot otherwise be clearly defined;

        b. The required level of effort is identified and agreed upon in advance;

        c. There is a reasonable assurance that the intended result cannot be achieved by expending less than the stipulated effort; and

        d. The contract price is $100,000 or less, unless approved by the chief of the contracting office.

B. Cost-Plus-Fixed-Fee-Term Form Contract (FAR 16.306(d))

    1. This type of contract is similar to the FFP/LOE contract, with the price equal to the cost incurred plus a fee. The contractor is required to perform at a stated level of effort over a specific period of time, but is not required to complete any specific work. This form of contract places all of the risk of performance and completion on the government.

C. Time-and-Materials Contracts (T&M) (FAR 16.601)

    1. Under a T&M contract, the government and the contractor negotiate fixed hourly or daily rates for labor. An estimated amount for other direct costs—such as materials, travel, equipment, etc.—is also negotiated. The work being acquired is

defined as a specified number of hours of effort by one or more individuals of a certain skill level. As the contract is performed, the contractor bills the actual hours or days incurred at the fixed hourly or daily rates specified for the categories of labor in the contract, and actual costs incurred for other direct costs.

2. Labor rates should be fully burdened (i.e., they should include indirect costs and profit). Materials are typically supplied at cost or catalog prices, and sometimes include a handling fee. Other direct costs may or may not be burdened with indirect costs and profit, depending on the terms of the contract.

3. A T&M contract is sometimes called a *fixed unit price* contract, but it is a type of flexibly priced contract since the number of hours/days—and therefore, the total contract amount—is not strictly fixed. Also, like a cost reimbursement–type contract, a contractor is not obligated to spend more money than the amount funded.

4. T&M and labor-hour contracts are used when it is impossible at the outset to estimate accurately the extent or duration of work or anticipate costs with any degree of confidence. Government monitoring is required, because the contractor has little incentive for cost control or labor efficiency. The contracting officer must prepare a determination and finding (D&F)

indicating that no other contract type is suitable. (FAR 16.601(d); *The Saxon Com.*, B-232694, Jan. 9, 1989, 89-1 CPD Par. 17.)

D. Labor-Hour Contracts (LH) (FAR 16.602)

1. A labor-hour contract is much like a T&M contract, except that other direct costs are not billable unless the contract specifically provides for it.

2. Under cost reimbursement and T&M–type contracts, costs incurred and billable under the contract may exceed estimated costs in the specific categories proposed, and the cost categories may be different from those proposed. But under an LH–type contract, the categories and types of other direct costs must be authorized under the contract. An LH contract is typically used when the government contracting officer wants to exercise control over other direct costs, especially travel.

3. Issues may arise concerning the proper billing level for subcontracted or "purchased" labor, particularly when a prime contractor is using several subcontractors that have different labor rates that also differ from the prime contractor's labor rates. This is discussed at length in FAR 52.232-7.

4. T&M or LH contracts may be used to acquire commercial items with certain restrictions, which are discussed in Unit 6.

5. In November 2008, the DOD extended the limitations imposed by the *FAR* on the use of T&M and LH contracts for commercial items to noncommercial DOD contracts as well. (DFARS 216.601.) A contracting officer may use a T&M or LH contract only when he or she has completed a D&F containing sufficient facts and rationale to justify that no other contract type is suitable. The contracting officer's D&F must

    a. Include a description of the market research conducted to determine what contract types are customary;

    b. Establish that it is not possible at the time to accurately estimate the extent or duration of the work or to anticipate costs with any reasonable degree of certainty;

    c. Establish that the requirement has been structured to maximize the use of fixed-price contracts on future procurements (e.g., by limiting the value or length of the T&M or LH contract); and

    d. If the acquisition involves an indefinite-delivery contract, the contracting officer must also structure the contract to allow the issuance of orders on a firm-fixed-price basis or fixed-price with economic price adjustment basis, or include additional explanation in the D&F as to why such alternative pricing arrangements are not practicable.

II. Indefinite-Delivery Contracts (FAR 16.5)

A. Indefinite-delivery contracts are characterized by the absence of a firm delivery date, and allow the government a greater degree of flexibility to order goods or services when the need arises.

  1. FAR 16.501-2(a) recognizes three types of indefinite-delivery contracts: definite quantity, requirements, and indefinite quantity.

  2. All three types permit government stocks to be maintained at minimum levels and permit direct shipment to users.

B. Definite-Quantity/Indefinite-Delivery Contracts (FAR 16.502; 52.216-20)

  1. The quantity and price are specified for a fixed period. When deliveries are needed, the government issues delivery orders that specify the delivery date and location.

  2. The contractor commits that supplies or services are available or will be made available within the contractually required delivery time.

C. Variable Quantity Contracts, Generally

  1. Variable quantity contracts permit flexibility in both quantities and delivery schedules. They permit ordering of supplies or services after requirements materialize.

2. A variable quantity contract must be either a requirements or an indefinitely delivery/ indefinite quantity (IDIQ) contract. *Satellite Services, Inc.*, B-280945.3, Dec. 4, 1998, 98-2 CPD Par. 125 (solicitation flawed where it neither guaranteed a minimum quantity, nor operated as a requirements contract).

3. Definitions (FAR 16.501-1)

   a. A *delivery order contract* is a contract for supplies that does not procure or specify a firm quantity of supplies (other than a minimum or maximum quantity) and that provides for the issuance of orders for the delivery of supplies during the period of the contract.

   b. A *task order contract* is a contract for services that does not procure or specify a firm quantity of services (other than a minimum or maximum quantity) and that provides for the issuance of orders for the performance of tasks during the period of the contract.

D. Requirements Contracts (FAR 16.503; 52.216-21)

   1. In a requirements contract, the government promises to order all of its requirements (however much they will be) from the contractor, and the contractor promises to fill all requirements. *Sea-Land Serv., Inc.*, B-266238, Feb. 8, 1996, 96-1 CPD Par. 49

(solicitation for requirements contract that contained a "Limitation of Government Liability" clause purporting to allow the government to order services elsewhere rendered contract illusory for lack of consideration).

   a. Diversion is a frequent issue. The government breaches the contract if it purchases its requirements from another source. *Torncello v. United States*, 681 F.2d 756 (Ct. Cl. 1982); *T&M Distributors, Inc.*, ABSCA No. 51279, 01-2 BCA Par. 31,442.

   b. The government also may breach the contract if it performs the contracted work in house. *C&S Park Serv., Inc.*, ENGBCA No. 3624, 78-1 BCA Par. 13,134 (failure to order mowing services in a timely fashion combined with use of government employees to perform mowing services entitled contractor to equitable adjustment under the changes clause).

   c. Contractors often seek lost profits as a measure of damages when the government purchases supplies or services from an outside source.

   d. Multiple-award (or nonexclusive) requirements contracts, where the government commits to more than one contractor, are not prohibited. See *Ace-Federal Reporters, Inc. v. Barram*, 226 F.3d 1329 (Fed. Cir. 2000); *GAP*

Instrument Corp., ASBCA No. 51658, 01-1 BCA Par. 31,358.

2. The contracting officer must state a realistic estimated total quantity in the solicitation and resulting contract. The estimate may be obtained from records of previous requirements and consumption, or by other means, and should be based on the most current information available. (FAR 16.503(a)(1))

   a. Failure to use available data or calculate the estimates with due care may entitle the contractor to additional compensation. See *Crown Laundry & Dry Cleaners v. United States*, 29 Fed. Cl. 506 (1993) (government negligent where estimates were exaggerated and not based on historical data); *Contract Management, Inc.*, ASBCA No. 44885, 95-2 BCA Par. 27,886 (relief under Changes clause where government failed to revise estimates between solicitation and award to reflect funding shortfalls).

   b. However, there is no obligation for the government to create or search for additional information. *Medart v. Austin*, 967 F.2d 579 (Fed. Cir. 1992) (court refused to impose a higher standard than imposed by regulations in finding reasonable the use of prior year's requirements as estimate).

   c. A variation of quantities clause (which entitles a party to an adjustment only if the actual work is greater or less than the estimated work by a given percentage) applies to situations where the workload deviates from the estimate due to facts that are not among those reasonably available to the estimator. *Womack v. United States*, 389 F.2d 793 (Ct. Cl. 1968). (negligent estimates entitle the contractor to additional compensation even if government attempts to limit its liability through use of variation of quantities clause); *Chemical Technology, Inc. v. United States*, 645 F.2d 934 (Ct. Cl. 1981) (failure to include requirements for reserve units on annual training in mess attendant services contract). An example of a variation in estimated quantity is the clause for fixed-price construction contracts at FAR 52.211-18, which provides that either party can seek an equitable adjustment if the actual work varies more than 15 percent above or below the contract estimate.

3. The only limitation on the government's freedom to vary its requirements after contract award is that it be done in good faith.

   a. The government acts in good faith if it has a valid business reason for varying its requirements, other than dissatisfaction with the contract. *Technical Assistance Int'l, Inc. v. United States*, 150 F.3d 1368 (Fed. Cir. 1998) (no breach or constructive change where government diminished need for vehicle maintenance and repair work by increasing the rate at which it added new vehicles into the installation fleet).

b. *Bad faith* includes actions motivated solely by a reassessment of the balance of the advantages and disadvantages under the contract such that the buyer decreases its requirements to avoid its obligations under the contract. *Technical Assistance Int'l, Inc. v. United States*, 150 F.3d 1368 (Fed. Cir. 1998) (citing *Empire Gas Com. v. American Bakeries Co.*, 840 F. 2d 1333, 1341 (7th Cir. 1988)).

c. The government is not liable for acts of God that cause a reduction in requirements. *Sentinel Protective Services. Inc.*, ASBCA No. 23560, 81-2 BCA Par. 15,194 (drought reduced need for grass cutting).

4. Advisory and Assistance Services. (FAR 16.503(d).) Advisory and assistance services are services provided under contract by nongovernmental sources to support or improve: organizational policy development, decision-making, management and administration, program and/or program management and administration, or research and development activities. (FAR 2.101) Activities may not issue solicitations for requirements contracts for advisory and assistance services in excess of three years and $10 million (including all options) unless the contracting officer determines in writing that the use of the multiple award procedures in FAR 16.504 is impracticable.

E. Indefinite-Quantity/Indefinite-Delivery Contracts (also called IDIQ or Minimum Quantity) (FAR 16.504)

1. An IDIQ contract requires the government to order and the contractor to furnish at least a stated minimum quantity of supplies or services. In addition, if ordered, the contractor shall furnish any additional quantities, not to exceed the stated maximum. (FAR 16.504(a)). The contract may also specify maximum or minimum quantities that may be ordered under each task or delivery order. (FAR 16.504(a)(3)).

2. The contract statement of work cannot be so broad as to be inconsistent with statutory authority for task order contracts and the requirements of the Competition in Contracting Act. *Valenzuela Engineering, Inc.*, B-277979, Jan. 26, 1998, 98-1 CPD Par. 51 (statement of work for operation and maintenance services at any government facility in the world deemed impermissibly broad).

3. In order for the contract to be binding, the minimum quantity in the contract must be more than a nominal quantity. FAR 16.504(a)(2). See *Sea-Land Serv., Inc.*, B278404.2 Feb. 9, 1998, 98-1 CPD Par. 47 (considering acquisition as a whole, guarantee of one "forty-foot equivalent unit" per contract carrier was adequate consideration to bind parties).

4. The contractor is entitled to receive only the guaranteed minimum. *Crown Laundry & Dry Cleaners, Inc.*, ASBCA No. 39982, 90-3 BCA Par. 22,993. See *Travel Centre v. Barram*, 236 F.3d 1316 (Fed. Cir. 2001) reversing *Travel Centre v. General Servs Admin*, GSBCA No. 14057, 98-1 BCA Par. 29,536 (COFC holds that government's order of minimum amount, even though the contractor was provided inaccurate estimates of expected orders, was legally sufficient).

5. The proper measure of damages for the government's failure to order the minimum quantity is not the full price of the unordered work, but the amount that the contractor lost as a result of the government's failure, such as lost profits. *AJT Assocs., Inc.*, ASBCA No. 50240, 97-1 BCA Par. 28,823 (contractor received lost profits on minimum amount); *Apex Int'l Mgmt. Servs., Inc.*, ASBCA No. 38087, 94-2 BCA Par. 26,842 (contractor entitled to be placed in as good a position as it would have been if the minimum quantity had been ordered).

6. FAR 16.504(a)(4) sets forth several requirements for indefinite-quantity solicitations and contracts, including the use of FAR 52.216-27, "Single or Multiple Awards;" and FAR 52.216-28, "Multiple Awards for Advisory and Assistance Services."

7. Where the government is buying services under an indefinite quantity–type contract, the government usually negotiates a fixed multiplier to be applied to the daily or hourly salaries of employees to be proposed later, or fixed daily or hourly rates. The fixed multiplier includes loading factors for indirect expenses (overhead, general and administrative expenses, etc.) and profit. The government then issues task orders for specific services. If the contract is designed to establish a fixed price for each task order, the contractor writes a proposal showing the employees proposed, their daily or hourly salaries times the multiplier negotiated previously, and the days or hours proposed for the task order. This proposal is then negotiated to establish a fixed price for the task order.

8. FAR 16.504(c) establishes a preference for making multiple awards of indefinite-quantity contracts under a single solicitation for similar supplies or services. The contracting officer must document the decision of whether or not to make multiple awards in the acquisition plan or contract file. See also DFARS 216.505.

a. A contracting officer must not make multiple awards if one or more of the conditions specified in FAR 16.504(c)(l)(ii)(B) are present.

  (1) Only one contractor is capable of providing performance at the level of quality required because the supplies or services are unique or highly specialized;

  (2) Based on the contracting officer's knowledge of the market, more favorable terms and conditions, including pricing, will be provided if a single award is made;

  (3) The cost of administration of multiple contracts may outweigh any potential benefits from making multiple awards;

  (4) The tasks likely to be ordered are so integrally related that only a single contractor can reasonably perform the work;

  (5) The total estimated value of the contract is less than the simplified acquisition threshold; or

  (6) Multiple awards would not be in the best interest of the government.

b. For advisory and assistance services contracts exceeding three years *and*

$11.5 million, including all options, the contracting officer must make multiple awards unless one or more of the following is true (FAR 16.504(c)(2)):

  (1) The contracting officer or other official designated by the head of the agency makes a written determination as part of acquisition planning that multiple awards are not practicable because only one contractor can reasonably perform the work because either the scope of work is unique or highly specialized, or the tasks so integrally related.

  (2) The contracting officer or other official designated by the head of the agency determines in writing, after the evaluation of offers, that only one offeror is capable of providing the services required at the level of quality required;

  (3) Only one offer is received; or

  (4) The contracting officer or other official designated by the head of the agency determines that the advisory and assistance services are incidental and not a significant component of the contract.

9. FAR 12.207 contains restrictions on the use of indefinite-delivery contracts for commercial items that are discussed in Unit 6.

10. Placing Orders (FAR 16.505)

   a. FAR 16.505(a) sets out the general requirements for orders under delivery or task-order contracts. A separate synopsis under FAR 5.201 is not required for orders.

   b. Orders under multiple award contracts. (FAR 16.505(b).)

      (1) Each awardee must be given a "fair opportunity to be considered for each order in excess of $2,500." See *Nations, Inc.*, B-272455, Nov. 5, 1996, 96-2 CPD Par. 170.

      (2) Exceptions: Awardees need not be given an opportunity to be considered for an order when any of the conditions described at FAR 16.505(b)(2) are present: urgent need, the existence of only one capable source, a logical follow-on order to a prior order issued after a fair opportunity was provided, or the need to issue the order to a particular contractor to satisfy a minimum guarantee.

      (3) Contracting officers have broad discretion in developing appropriate order placement procedures. Procedures should be tailored to each acquisition. Submission requirements should be kept to a minimum.

   The contracting officer must not employ allocation or designation of any preferred awardee(s) that would result in less than fair consideration being given to all awardees prior to placing each order.

      (4) The contracting officer makes his or her determination based on past performance, quality of delivery, cost, and other factors the contracting officer believes are relevant. Price or cost is a mandatory factor in the selection process. Formal evaluation plans and scoring of offers or quotes are not required.

      (5) The contracting officer must document in the contract file the rationale for placement and price of each order.

11. Protests Concerning Orders

   a. The issuance of a task or delivery order is protestable to the Government Accountability Office if the order is valued in excess of $10 million, or if the protest is based on the grounds that the order increases the scope, period, or maximum value of the contract under which the order is issued. (U.S.C. § 2304c(e).)

   b. An order can also be protested if it is serving as a downselection, or if the competition is held between an IDIQ contractor or blanket purchase agreement (BPA) holder, and another vendor.

   c. The *FAR* requires the head of an agency to designate a task and delivery order ombudsman to review complaints from contractors and ensure they are afforded a fair opportunity to be considered for orders. The ombudsman must be a senior agency official independent of the contracting officer and may be the agency's competition advocate. (FAR 16.505(b)(5).)

III. Letter Contracts (FAR 16.603)

A. A letter contract is awarded when the government needs the goods or services immediately and a complete contract cannot be negotiated in sufficient time to meet that need. Letter contracts are used to expedite performance in exigent or emergency circumstances, and are not to be used to compensate for poor planning.

B. A letter contract is a written preliminary contractual instrument that authorizes the contractor to begin performance immediately. It includes some terms and conditions, but not all. One missing term is usually the total contract price. To reimburse the contractor for costs incurred before the price is negotiated, the government appropriates some money. The dollar figure allotted, known as a not-to-exceed (NTE) amount, is usually very low. However, it can be increased if the contractor

and the government do not agree upon a price before the money is used up.

C. Letter contracts must be approved for use by the Head of the Contracting Activity (HCA), or designee, before award. (FAR 16.603-3; DFARS 217.7404-1(a).) Approved letter contracts must include an NTE price.

D. Definitization. The parties must reduce the contract terms to writing within 180 days after issuance or before completion of 40 percent of the work, whichever comes first. (10 U.S.C. § 2326; FAR 16.603-2(c); DFARS Subpart 217.7404-3(a)(1).) Until the contract terms are definitized, the government may not pay the contractor more than 50 percent of the NTE price. (FAR 16.603-2(d); DFARS 217.7404-4.) If the parties cannot reach agreement, the letter agreement can be unilaterally definitized by the contracting officer, subject to the disputes clause.

IV. Basic Agreements/Basic Ordering Agreements (FAR 16.7)

A. Basic agreements (BAs) and basic ordering agreements (BOAs) are not contracts.

B. Rather, they are written instruments of understanding that:

   1. Contain clauses applying to future contracts between the parties during its term; and

   2. Contemplate separate future contracts that will incorporate by reference (or

attachment) required and applicable clauses agreed upon in the basic agreement.

C. BAs and BOAs are used when a substantial number of separate contracts may be awarded and significant recurring negotiating problems have been experienced with the contractor.

D. BAs and BOAs may be used with negotiated fixed-price or cost-reimbursement contracts.

V. OPTIONS (FAR 17.2)

A. An option is a unilateral right in a contract by which, for a specified time, the government may elect to purchase additional supplies or services called for by the contract, or may elect to extend the contract. (FAR 2.101.)

B. Total Contract Period

1. Generally, a contract, including all options, may not exceed five years. (FAR 17.204(e)). This time limitation does not apply to information technology contracts.

2. Variable option periods do not restrict competition. *Madison Services, Inc.*, B-278962, Apr. 17, 1998, 98-1 CPD Par. 113 (Navy's option clause that allowed the Navy to vary the length of the option period from one to twelve months did not unduly restrict competition).

C. Unpriced Options: Unpriced options, and other agreements to agree, are enforceable if conditioned upon an obligation to bargain in good faith. *Aviation Contractor Employees,*

Inc. v. United States, 945 F.2d 1568 (Fed. Cir. 1991). Otherwise, they are unenforceable. Restatement (Second) Contracts, § 33 (1981).

D. Exercising Options

1. The government must comply with applicable statutes and regulations before exercising an option. (FAR 17.207.) *Golden West Refining Co.*, EBCA No. C-9208134, 94-3 BCA Par. 27,184 (option exercise invalid because statute required award to bidder under a new procurement); *New England Tank Indus. of N.H., Inc.*, ASBCA No. 26474, 90-2 BCA Par. 22,892 (option exercise invalid because of agency's failure to follow DOD regulation by improperly obligating stock funds).

a. The contracting officer may exercise an option only after determining that

(1) Funds are available. (Note that failure to determine that funds are available does not render an option exercise ineffective—it relates to an internal matter and does not create rights for contractors.) *United Food Servs., Inc.*, ASBCA No. 43711, 93-1 BCA Par. 25,462 (holding valid the exercise of a one-year option subject to availability of funds);

(2) The requirement fills an existing need;

(3) The exercise of the option is the most advantageous method of fulfilling the government's need, price, and other factors considered; and

(4) The option was synopsized in accordance with FAR Part 5 unless exempted under that part.

b. The contracting officer shall make the determination to exercise the option on the basis of one of the following:

(1) A new solicitation fails to produce a better price or more advantageous offer;

(2) An informal analysis of the market indicates that the option is more advantageous; or

(3) The time between contract award and exercise of the option is so short that exercising the option is most advantageous.

2. The government must exercise the option according to its terms. See *Lockheed Martin Corp. v. Walker,* 149 F.3d 1377 (Fed. Cir. 1998) (the government wrongfully exercised options out of sequence); *VARO, Inc.,* ASBCA No. 47945, 96-1 BCA Par. 28,161 (inclusion of eight additional contract clauses in option exercise invalidated the option); *The Boeing Co.,* ASBCA No. 37579, 90-3 BCA Par. 23,202 (Navy failed to exercise the option within the 60 days allowed in the contract and the court invalidated the option).

3. If a contractor contends that an option was exercised improperly, and performs, it may be entitled to an equitable adjustment. See *Lockheed Martin IR Imaging Systems, Inc. v. West,* 108 F.3d 319 (1997) (partial exercise of an option was held to be a constructive change to the contract).

4. The government has the discretion to decide whether to exercise an option.

a. The decision to exercise an option is subject to protest. *Alice Roofing & Sheet Metal Works, Inc.,* B-283153, Oct. 13, 1999, 99-2 CPD Par. 70 (protest denied where agency reasonably determined that option exercise was most advantageous means of satisfying needs).

b. The decision not to exercise an option, however, is generally not a protestable issue since it involves a matter of contract administration.

c. A contractor may file a claim under the Disputes clause. See *KirklMarsland Advertising, Inc.,* ASBCA No., 51075, 99-2 Par. 30,439 (summary judgment to government on contractor claim of bad faith or abuse of discretion); *Pennyrile Plumbing, Inc.,* ASBCA No. 44555, 96-1 BCA Par. 28,044 (no bad faith or abuse of discretion).

UNIT 06

Special Types of Acquisitions

Contract Types

I. Commercial Item Contracting

A. FAR Part 12 implements the government's preference for the acquisition of commercial items, as stated in the Federal Acquisition Streamlining Act of 1994 (Public Law 103-355). This acquisition method was implemented (1) to streamline government acquisition to make it more "commercial-like," and (b) to increase government access to commercial companies that were reluctant to subject themselves to the full panoply of government contract regulations. FAR 12.101 provides that agencies should

1. Conduct market research to determine whether commercial items or nondevelopmental items are available to meet the agency's requirements.

2. Acquire commercial items or nondevelopmental items when they are available to meet the needs of the agency; and

3. Require prime contractors and subcontractors at all tiers to incorporate, to the maximum extent practicable, commercial items or nondevelopmental items into components of items supplied to the agency.

B. As defined in FAR 2.101, a *commercial item* is

1. An item that has been sold, leased, or licensed to the general public;

2. An item that has been offered for sale, lease, or license to the general public;

3. An item with standard modifications (or nonstandard modifications) is available in the commercial marketplace;

4. A service that is

   a. Procured in support of a commercial item; or

   b. Of a type of commercial service that is commonly sold to the general public through the use of T&M and LH contracts; and

5. Also a category that includes some types of nondevelopmental items (NDIs).

C. Commercial item contracting under FAR Part 12 allows for streamlined contract administration:

1. The Cost Accounting Standards (CAS) do not apply,

2. Many certification requirements and compliance rules do not apply, and

3. There are only a limited number of mandatory flowdown clauses.

D. A DOD Major Weapon System may be treated as a commercial item, or acquired under FAR Part 12, only if

1. The Secretary of Defense determines that

   a. The major weapon system is a commercial item as defined in FAR 2.101;

b. Such treatment is necessary to meet national security objectives; and

c. The offeror has submitted sufficient information to evaluate, through price analysis, the reasonableness of the price for the system;

2. Congressional defense committees are notified at least 30 days in advance; and

3. A subsystem that meets the definition of a commercial item may be acquired as a commercial item only if the major weapon system is being acquired under Part 12.

E. FAR 12.207 specifies the permissible contract types for use in commercial item acquisitions.

1. Two types of contracts can be used to acquire commercial product equipment and services:

   a. Firm-fixed-price contracts, and

   b. Fixed-price contracts with economic price adjustments.

2. Indefinite-delivery contracts may be used in very limited circumstances.

3. Time-and-materials contracts and labor-hour contracts may be used in very limited circumstances.

4. The use of any other contract type to acquire commercial items is prohibited.

5. These contract types may be used in conjunction with an award fee and performance or delivery incentives only when the award fee or incentive is based solely on factors other than cost (FAR 16.202-1, 16.203-1). Common non-cost incentives include (FAR 16.402-2 and 16.402-3)

   a. Performance incentives, which are designed to relate profit objectives to the results achieved by the contractor compared to certain specified targets; and

   b. Delivery incentives, which specify rewards and/or penalties to promote improvements from a required delivery schedule.

F. An agency may use a T&M or LH contract to acquire commercial items only when it has completed a determination and finding (D&F) containing sufficient facts and rationale to justify that a firm-fixed-pricing arrangement is not suitable. Specifically,

1. The commercial services must be acquired under competitive procedures, procedures other than full and open competition, or where the contractors have been given fair opportunity to be considered.

2. The contracting officer must

   a. Execute a D&F stating that no other contract type authorized by FAR 12.207 is suitable,

    b.   Include a ceiling price in the contract that the contractor exceeds at its own risk, and

    c.   Authorize any subsequent change to that ceiling price only upon a determination that it is in the best interests of the procuring activity to change that price.

3.   The contracting officer's D&F must

    a.   Include a description of the market research conducted to determine what contract types are customary;

    b.   Establish that it is not possible at the time to accurately estimate the extent or duration of the work or to anticipate costs with any reasonable degree of certainty; and

    c.   Establish that the requirement has been structured to maximize the use of fixed-price contracts on future procurements (e.g., by limiting the value or length of the T&M or LH contract).

4.   If the acquisition involves an indefinite-delivery contract, the contracting officer must also structure the contract to allow the issuance of orders on a firm-fixed-price basis or fixed-price with economic price adjustment basis, or include additional explanations in the D&F as to why such alternative pricing arrangements are not practicable.

G. Indefinite-delivery contracts may be used only when

    1.   Unit prices are established based on a firm-fixed-price or a fixed-price with economic price adjustment, or

    2.   Rates are established for commercial services acquired on a time-and-materials or labor-hour basis.

II. Performance-based Contracting (FAR 37.6)

A. A performance-based acquisition is defined as an acquisition structured around the results to be achieved as opposed to the manner by which the work is to be performed (FAR 2.101). Performance-based contracting methods are intended to ensure that required performance quality levels are achieved and that total payment is related to the degree that services performed meet contract standard.

B. Performance-based acquisitions emphasize the use of measurable performance and quality criteria in lieu of more specific or "how to" work statements.

    1.   They place a greater reliance on performance work statements (PWSs) and statements of objectives (SOOs), rather than detailed specifications and statements of work.

    2.   Work performance is assessed against measurable performance standards.

3. Financial incentives encourage innovative and cost-effective performance.

C. The Services Acquisition Reform Act encourages government officials to use performance-based service contracts (PBSCs) by allowing procurement officials to treat certain solicitations for PBSCs as commercial item acquisitions under FAR Part 12. (169 Pub. L. No. 108-136. §§ 1411-1443, (2003)).

D. Contracting officers are directed to use the following order of precedence:

1. A firm-fixed-price performance-based contract or task order,

2. A performance-based contract or task order that is not firm-fixed price, and then

3. A contract or task order that is not performance-based.

E. Properly structured performance-based contracts have many benefits for the government, including

1. Increased likelihood of meeting mission needs;

2. Better value and enhanced performance;

3. Less performance risk;

4. The elimination of detailed specifications or process descriptions;

5. Contractor flexibility in proposing solutions;

6. Better competition;

7. Contractor buy-in and shared interests, which permit innovation and cost effectiveness;

8. Less likelihood of a successful bid protest;

9. Less frequent, but more meaningful contractor surveillance; and

10. Results documented for the Government Performance and Results Act reporting.

F. Another limitation on the use of overly descriptive specification requirements is found in FAR Part 39's prohibition against solicitations for information technology services that describe any minimum experience or educational requirement for proposed contractor personnel, unless the contracting officer determines that the needs of the agency

1. Cannot be met without that requirement, or

2. Require the use of other than a performance-based contract under FAR 37.6.

G. Performance-based contracts should include (FAR 37.602)

1. A statement of work that clearly defines requirements and

a. States *what* (outcome), not *how* (method);

b. Contains measurable performance standards (terms of quality, timeliness, quantity, etc.); and

c. Uses a PWS or an SOW;

2. Quality assurance/surveillance procedures (FAR 46.103(a) and 46.401);

3. Selection procedures; and

4. Performance incentives, where appropriate (FAR 37.601)

   a. Incentives should correspond to the performance standards in the contract's PWS/SOO. (FAR 16.402-2)

   b. Incentive-type contracts used for performance-based service acquisitions may include both fixed-price and cost-reimbursement contracts, and both incentive-fee and award-fee contracts.

H. Guidance on performance-based services acquisition can be found in several places:

1. The Office of Federal Procurement Policy's October 1998, *Guide to Best Practices for Performance-based Service Contracting."*[1]

2. The Department of Commerce web-based virtual guide, launched in 2002, titled, *"Seven Steps to Performance-based Services Acquisition."*[2]

Endnotes

1. At time of publication, this could be found at **www. whitehouse.gov/omb/rewrite/procurement/pbsa/ guide_pbsc.html**.

2. At time of publication, this could be found at **https://www.acquisition.gov/comp/seven_steps/ home.html**.

UNIT 02

Today and Tomorrow

Contract Types

I. Office of Management and Budget Guidelines

A. On October 27, 2009, the Office of Management and Budget (OMB) issued guidelines instructing agencies to reduce by at least 10 percent the amount obligated to new noncompetitive, cost-reimbursement or T&M/LH contracts. (See Appendix A.)

These instructions were based on

1. A Presidential Memorandum, dated March 4, 2009, describing concerns with recent trends in outsourcing, cost-reimbursement contracting, and insufficient competition. (Office of Federal Procurement Policy Briefing Room, Presidential Memorandum on Government Contracting.) (See Appendix B.)

2. Instructions issued by OMB in July 2009, "Improving Government Acquisition," Office of Management and Budget (M-09-25, July 29, 2009). (See Appendix C.)

3. The Office of Federal Procurement Policy (which is part of OMB) will use these guidelines to evaluate agencies semi-annually in FY2010 and 2011 on the extent to which they have reduced their "high risk" contracting vehicles.

B. The OMB guidelines focused on three questions:

1. How is the agency maximizing the effective use of competition and choosing the best contract type for the acquisition?

2. How is the agency mitigating risk when noncompetitive, cost-reimbursement, or time-and-materials/labor-hour contracts are used?

3. How is the agency creating opportunities to transition to more competitive or lower risk contracts?

C. OMB made the following suggestions for maximizing the effective use of competition and choosing the best contract type:

1. Develop requirements with sufficient information in the statements of work and sufficient response time to allow contractors to make informed decisions about whether to bid.

2. Gather information from industry and ensure that contracting officers understand the market.

3. Use performance-based acquisition for acquiring services.

4. Use existing contracts rather than conducting new competitions.

5. Make sure task order and delivery order contracts have consistent emphasis on competition.

6. Encourage maximum consideration of small businesses.

7. Prefer fixed-price contracts; use cost-reimbursement contracts only when there

is uncertainty about the resources that will be necessary to achieve the government's objectives.

8. Convert cost contracts to fixed-price when, over time, that uncertainty is removed.

9. Use incentive payments to encourage cost control and on-time performance.

D. OMB made the following suggestions for mitigating risk when noncompetitive, cost-reimbursement or T&M/LH contracts are used:

1. Limit the performance period of the contract.

2. Follow FAR Part 15 requirements to ensure price reasonableness.

3. Regularly assess contractor performance.

4. Submit performance assessments to the Past Performance Information Retrieval System (PPIRS).

5. Increase oversight of contractor accounting systems and cost controls.

6. Link payment to quality, efficiency, and timeliness of performance on award-fee contracts.

7. Ensure that acquisition professionals have sufficient skills to manage cost-type contracts.

8. Pay attention to justifications for using T&M/LH contracts for commercial items acquisitions.

E. OMB made the following suggestions for creating opportunities to transition to more competitive or lower risk contracts:

1. Contact contractors that express interest in a solicitation but do not submit offers, to understand why they decided not to participate.

2. Perform spend analysis of their largest spend categories to find out if other practices might result in greater competition.

3. Implement contract review boards, peer reviews, or contract type advocates in determining which contract types to employee.

4. Use hybrid contracts where possible, in which some requirements are addressed through fixed-price payments, and cost-reimbursable or T&M/LH contracting is used for only a small number of requirements.

II. DOD Guidance Regarding Award Fees

A. On March 29, 2006, DOD issued a memorandum regarding the proper use of award fees. (See Appendix D.)

1. Award fees should be tied to identifiable interim outcomes and structured to motivate contractors.

2. "Rollover" award fees (i.e., award-fee plans that allow unawarded portions of the award-fee pool to be moved to award-fee pools for future periods) should be the exception, rather than the rule.

B. In a subsequent memorandum issued on May 24, 2007, DOD requires

   1. The use of objective measurable standards that mean something to the program,

   2. Setting a specific percentage for specific ratings, and

   3. Making the maximum award fee available only if contractor exceeds standards.

C. A December 2007 OMB best practices memorandum includes these recommendations, and also reminds contracting officers to consider administrative costs as well. (See Appendix E.)

APPENDIX A

Increasing Competition and Structuring Contracts for the Best Results

OFFICE OF FEDERAL
PROCUREMENT POLICY

EXECUTIVE OFFICE OF THE PRESIDENT
OFFICE OF MANAGEMENT AND BUDGET
WASHINGTON, D.C. 20503

October 27, 2009

MEMORANDUM FOR CHIEF ACQUISITION OFFICERS
SENIOR PROCUREMENT EXECUTIVES

FROM: Lesley A. Field
             Deputy Administrator

SUBJECT: Increasing Competition and Structuring Contracts for the Best Results

The President's March 4, 2009, Memorandum on Government Contracting calls on federal agencies to examine their use of noncompetitive and cost-reimbursement contracting as one of several key actions to improve results achieved from government contractors. Each of these contracting authorities carries significant potential risk of overspending taxpayer resources. Noncompetitive contracts place agencies in the position of having to negotiate contracts without the benefit of a direct market mechanism to help establish pricing. Competitions that yield only one offer in response to a solicitation deprive agencies of the ability to consider alternative solutions in a reasoned and structured manner. Cost-reimbursement contracts, as well as time-and-materials and labor-hour (T&M/LH) contracts, provide limited direct incentive to control costs. Reports from the Government Accountability Office (GAO), agency inspectors general, and agency management point to a general overuse of these authorities and significant lost opportunities for savings and performance efficiencies.

To address these concerns, the Office of Management and Budget (OMB) instructed agencies to take immediate action. In accordance with OMB Memorandum M-09-25, *Improving Government Acquisition* (July 29, 2009), agencies must reduce by at least 10 percent the combined share of dollars obligated through new contracts in FY 2010 that are: (1) awarded non-competitively and/or receive only one bid in response to a solicitation or a request for quote, (2) cost-reimbursement contracts, or (3) T&M/LH contracts.

The President's Memorandum also called upon OMB to issue guidance: (1) to govern the appropriate use and oversight of sole-source and other types of noncompetitive contracts and to maximize the use of full and open competition and other competitive procurement processes; and (2) to govern the appropriate use and oversight of all contract types, in full consideration of the agency's needs, and to minimize risk and maximize the value of Government contracts generally.

In response to the President's charge, the Office of Federal Procurement Policy (OFPP) has established initial guidelines to help Chief Acquisition Officers (CAOs) and Senior Procurement Executives (SPEs) evaluate the effectiveness of their agency's competition practices and processes for selecting contract types. The guidelines focus around three key questions:

(1) How is the agency maximizing the effective use of competition and choosing the best contract type for the acquisition?

(2) How is the agency mitigating risk when noncompetitive, cost-reimbursement, or T&M/LH contracts are used?

(3) How is the agency creating opportunities to transition to more competitive and lower risk contracts?

OFPP's guidelines include a set of considerations to help CAOs and SPEs address each of these questions. They are intended to help agencies identify specific areas in need of greater management attention, training, and workforce development. Accordingly, CAOs and SPEs should use the considerations to evaluate progress against their high risk contracting reduction targets. These evaluations may be included as part the competition advocate's annual assessment of agency accomplishments and planned actions. The evaluations may also be coordinated with reviews performed pursuant to OFPP's *Guidelines for Assessing the Acquisition Function*[1], which integrate acquisition reviews with the internal control procedures outlined in OMB Circular A-123. OFPP will review progress against the targets on a semiannual basis in FY 2010 and require corrective action plans, where necessary. OFPP will set new targets for FY 2011 and beyond and work with agencies to identify best practices, new techniques and strategies, areas in need of additional guidance or policy, and measures and benchmarks.

To achieve sustained improvement, OFPP will work with CAOs, SPEs, and competition advocates to identify and share best practices, new techniques and strategies, areas in need of additional guidance or policy, measures and benchmarks. These efforts will include review and refinement, as appropriate, of the initial considerations to enhance their value as a tool for identifying opportunities for improvement.

Achieving good results from contracting tools is directly linked to the skills, judgment, and capacity of the acquisition workforce. These skills and judgments must be especially well honed to meet the heightened challenges associated with high-risk contracting. OFPP is working with the Defense Acquisition University (DAU) and the Federal Acquisition Institute (FAI) to identify areas in need of targeted training and opportunities for rapidly communicating with the affected community as new rules and policies are developed. CAOs and SPEs should actively identify training needs within their community and aggressively leverage the available training resources of DAU and FAI. Agencies should also review OFPP's Acquisition Workforce Development Strategic Plan[2] to consider their workforce needs.

OFPP appreciates the attention your agency is giving to the President's Memorandum. We look forward to working with your staff and sharing the best practices they develop to increase savings, reduce high-risk contracting, and improve the value our taxpayers receive from federal contracts. Questions regarding this memorandum may be directed to Mathew Blum at (202) 395-4953 or mblum@omb.eop.gov.

Attachment

---

[1] See OFPP Memorandum, *Guidelines for Assessing the Acquisition Function* (May 21, 2008), available at http://www.whitehouse.gov/omb/assets/omb/procurement/memo/a123_guidelines.pdf.

[2] See OFPP Memorandum, *Acquisition Workforce Development Strategic Plan for Civilian Agencies* – FYs 2010-2014.

Contract Types

Guidelines for Increasing Competition
and Structuring Contracts for the Best Results

The President's March 4, 2009, Memorandum on Government Contracting directs agencies to strengthen their use of competition and improve how contracts are structured. The Memorandum states, in particular, that agencies must strive for a process that is "open and competitive" when awarding government contracts. Competition lies at the heart of the federal acquisition system. It drives down costs, motivates better contractor performance, helps to curb fraud and waste, and promotes innovation.

The President's Memorandum further states that government contracts should be structured to "minimize risk and maximize value" for the taxpayer. In most cases, fixed-price contracts will be best suited for achieving this goal because they provide the contractor with the greatest incentive for efficient and economical performance. In circumstances where there is considerable uncertainty regarding the requirements, however, cost-reimbursement contracts or, in more limited circumstances, time-and-materials or labor-hour (T&M/LH) contracts may provide for a more effective allocation of risk between the government and the contractor.

OFPP has established initial guidelines to help Chief Acquisition Officers (CAOs) and Senior Procurement Executives evaluate the effectiveness of their competition practices and processes for selecting contract types. The guidelines should be used to help agencies achieve their targets for reducing the use of high risk contracting authorities. OFPP will review progress against the targets on a semiannual basis in FY 2010 and require corrective action plans, where necessary. OFPP will set new targets for FY 2011 and beyond and work with agencies to identify best practices, new techniques and strategies, areas in need of additional guidance or policy, and measures and benchmarks.

The guidelines consist of *three key questions* and a set of *considerations* for addressing each question. The purpose of the considerations, many of which have been drawn from basic tenets of acquisition policy, is to help identify specific areas in need of greater management attention, training, and workforce development. OFPP will consider refinements to the guidelines based on agency experience.

Key Question #1

How is the agency maximizing the effective use of competition and choosing the best contract type for the acquisition?

Initial considerations

A. Maximizing the effective use of competition

1. **Focus on requirements development and outreach to potential vendors**. Poorly developed requirements that are either vague or unduly restrictive are detrimental to meaningful competition. To promote competition effectively, agencies must provide sufficient information in the statement of work and sufficient time for response. These steps will allow offerors to make informed business decisions on whether to respond to a solicitation and work with end users to perform the due diligence necessary to propose the best solutions. Agencies should take appropriate steps to ensure contracting and program offices are working together and applying their respective skill sets to understand the market for the types of products or services they need, including how industry is structured (e.g., how distribution channels function), potential cost drivers (e.g., how services are provided), and its competitive state. These collaborative efforts would include:

   - inviting potential offerors, through a request for information or an industry day that provides a general description of the scope or purpose of the acquisition, to submit information or have discussions on marketplace capabilities;

   - taking advantage of the full range of market research tools to understand marketplace capabilities and identify all reasonable potential solutions; and

   - engaging potential suppliers, whenever practicable, in an advisory process, especially for complex needs, such as major systems, that invites potential offerors, through a pre-solicitation notice, to submit information that the agency would evaluate to advise offerors of their potential to be viable competitors. An advisory process enables potential vendors to more wisely use their internal resources to perform due diligence.

   By applying both contracting and program skills on these efforts, agencies can facilitate the development of informative requirements documents with expected levels of service quality that put offerors in the best position to propose to the agency's actual needs. This, in turn, increases the probability of awarding a contract through competition that represents the best value available in, or capable of being developed by, the marketplace.

2. **Use performance based acquisitions and commercial solutions**. Performance-based acquisition (PBA) is the government's preferred approach for acquiring services. PBA principles call on agencies to focus on mission outcomes, rather than prescriptions for how work is to be performed or key personnel requirements. By emphasizing this approach, agencies can encourage meaningful competition by allowing vendors to offer more innovative solutions to meet the agency's

performance needs. PBA also allows vendors to offer market-tested commercial solutions at competitive pricing with risks that can be reasonably managed by a small or large business under a fixed-price contract.

3. **Evaluate alternative competition strategies for larger and more complex requirements**. Agencies should ensure that, as part of market research and acquisition planning processes, their contracting and program offices are working together to consider the comparative benefits of awarding a new contract using full and open competition versus placing an order under an existing contract. In making this comparison, agencies might evaluate the strength of each competition strategy in terms of its ability to (i) generate meaningful competition, (ii) meet needs in a timely manner, and (iii) allow for the negotiation of fair and reasonable pricing and terms and conditions to address the requirements at hand.

4. **Use strategic sourcing**. Agencies should actively consider the use of strategic sourcing when requirements can be satisfied through a contracting vehicle under the Federal Strategic Sourcing Initiative. These vehicles have been established to maximize the value of competition by using the government's buying leverage. If these contracting vehicles are not used and the agency chooses instead to use its own vehicle, such as an enterprise-wide vehicle, managers should ensure their agency documents in the contract file the reasons for doing so (e.g., describe the greater savings and/or the more favorable terms and conditions anticipated).[1]

5. **Ensure consistent maximization of competition at the task and delivery order level**. Reviews by agency management, the GAO, and agency IGs indicate that use of competition on task and delivery order contracts is inconsistent. At the same time, data from the Federal Procurement Data System (FPDS) shows that agency expenditures through orders under contracts has increased from just 14 percent of dollars obligated in FY 1990 to more than half of total obligated dollars in FY 2008. These shortcomings coupled with the increasing level of obligations through these vehicles warrant greater management attention by agencies to ensure agencies are achieving meaningful competition in their placement of task and delivery orders, such as by:

   • applying greater competitive rigor through the disclosure of significant factors and subfactors and their relative importance when conducting the "fair opportunity process" for orders over $5 million; and

   • using data generated by new FPDS reports to evaluate in new competitions the extent to which task and delivery order competition is being achieved.

6. **Give maximum practicable consideration to small businesses, including minority businesses, and businesses owned by women and veterans**. In order to maximize performance and minimize

---

[1] CFO Act agencies are strongly encouraged to prepare as part of (or supplement) their acquisition savings plan to identify (a) their estimated department annual obligations for strategically sourced products or services (e.g., express ground delivery, software and maintenance services, and plumbing and electrical services), (b) the estimated obligation amount to be strategically sourced in FY 10 and 11 and (c) reasons why a strategic sourcing vehicle was not used for all of the agency's spend for that requirement.

costs, agencies need to consider the full range of possible suppliers. Small businesses provide creativity, innovation, and technical expertise to support a wide range of agency requirements at good prices, but are sometimes overlooked as suppliers. Agencies should take appropriate steps to facilitate regular collaboration of contracting and program offices with their Offices of Small and Disadvantaged Business Utilization (OSDBU) in planning acquisitions to identify: (1) requirements that can be met effectively with the help of small businesses, and (2) the small business contracting authority that is best suited for a given requirement and will help the government meet and exceed its small business contracting goals. OSDBUs, the Small Business Administration's (SBA) District Offices, and the Department of Commerce's Minority Business Development Agency can assist agencies with market research to help identify qualified and capable small business sources for prime contracting and subcontracting, both at the national and local level. OSDBUs should actively share their strategies for facilitating access to federal business opportunities. SBA's Procurement Advisory Council serves as one forum for OSDBU exchanges.

B. Choosing the best contract type for the acquisition

1. **Determine the level of uncertainty**. Determining whether an agency should award a fixed-price, cost-reimbursement, or T&M/LH contract requires careful consideration of the level of uncertainty regarding the agency's requirements.

   Fixed-price contracts are preferred unless uncertainty in the requirement and the risk of failure cannot be managed by the contractor within economically reasonable bounds. Fixed-price contracts provide greater incentive than cost-reimbursement contracts for the contractor to control costs and perform efficiently. Many of the same practices that facilitate meaningful competition also promote fixed-price contracting. Sound requirements development and performance-based statements of work, for example, give contractors the opportunity to understand the government's needs and offer solutions, including market-tested commercial items, with an amount of risk that they can manage for a fixed price.

   Cost-reimbursement contracts are more appropriate when there is considerable uncertainty about the resources that will be necessary to achieve the government's objective. This uncertainty may be due to lack of knowledge regarding the effort needed to meet a defined requirement, including a lack of cost experience in performing the work. Alternatively, the uncertainty may be due more fundamentally to a lack of knowledge about what is possible and practical, as is often the case with research or leading-edge innovation. Similarly, T&M/LH contracts may help agencies accomplish tasks for a reasonable cost where the needed amount of labor effort cannot be specified in advance, such as for emergency repair services. In these situations, a cost reimbursement or T&M/LH contract allows the government to absorb a greater portion of the risk and avoid the costly contingencies that contractors would pass on to taxpayers if forced to offer their services on a fixed-price basis.[2]

---

[2] FAR changes are in process to improve policies and practices associated with the use of cost-reimbursement contracting and help to guard against their overuse. Changes will address: (1) when and under what circumstances cost-reimbursement contracts are appropriate, (2) the acquisition plan findings necessary to support a decision to use cost-reimbursement contracts, and (3) the acquisition workforce resources necessary to award and manage cost-reimbursement contracts.

Over time, experience should generally enable the agency to address these uncertainties, making it possible to convert to a fixed-price contract that creates a better incentive to provide the desired products or services within time and on budget.

2. **Use incentives to motivate lower costs with improved delivery or technical performance and to discourage contractor inefficiency and waste**. In cost-type contracting, incentives enable the government to reduce its exposure to risk by tying the payment of fees to contractor performance. During acquisition planning, agencies should consider the type of incentive that is most likely to motivate efficient and economical performance. For example, the agency should consider use of an objective incentive fee when cost and performance targets can be predetermined and a formula can be used to adjust the negotiated fee based on variations relative to objective targets. The agency might consider an award fee if it is neither feasible nor effective to devise predetermined objective incentives for cost, technical performance, or schedule.

Incentive arrangements should be developed through close collaboration between the contracting officer, program manager, and technical requirements staff. Incentives should be considered not only to motivate good cost control but also to encourage quality on-time performance, taking into consideration factors that are within the contractor's control, such as achieving a delivery or test schedule, application of quality controls, and effective implementation of maintenance requirements.

Key Question #2

How is the agency mitigating risk when noncompetitive, cost-reimbursement, or time-and-materials / labor-hour contracts are used?

Initial considerations

A. Mitigating the risk of noncompetitive contracts

1. **Limit the length of the contract**. Noncompetitive contracts play an important role in helping agencies address requirements that can only be satisfied by one source or that rise during emergencies when time allows only limited consideration of offers. But these contracts carry risk of overspending because they have been negotiated without the benefit of a direct market mechanism. One way to mitigate risk is to limit the contract's performance period. In some cases, limitations are imposed by law and/or regulation. For example, in circumstances of unusual and compelling urgency, FAR 6.302-2 states that the total period of performance shall not exceed the minimum period necessary for meeting the unusual and compelling urgency requirements, but no longer than one year or such period as specified in law, unless a longer period for performance is approved by the head of the contracting activity. [3] Such approval is in addition to that provided as part of the initial decision to make an award using other than full and open competition.

2. **Ensure price reasonableness**. Agencies must ensure fair and reasonable pricing on all of their acquisitions. This requirement can present challenges when adequate price competition is lacking. Agencies should ensure agencies are obtaining the information and data they need, consistent with the policies established in FAR Subpart 15.4. The FAR Council is currently reviewing proposed clarifications to the pricing policies in FAR Subpart 15.4 regarding the circumstances and procedures for obtaining data or information in the absence of adequate price competition to establish the reasonableness of offered prices.

3. **Regularly assess contractor performance**. Regular assessment and reporting of the contractor's quality, timeliness, cost control, and concern for the customer will improve the agency's ability to motivate quality contractor performance during the life of a contract, including one that has been awarded noncompetitively. The contractor will be motivated by the fact that the strength of its performance on the current contract could affect its position when competing for future federal work.

---

[3] The Department of Homeland Security and its components are limited to a period of performance no longer than 150 days unless a longer period of performance is approved by the head of the contracting activity.

FAR Subpart 42.15 requires regular assessment of contractor performance and submission of electronic records of these assessments in the Past Performance Information Retrieval System (PPIRS) so that the information may be considered by other agencies. Beginning in February 2010, OFPP will conduct regular compliance assessments and quality reviews to make certain that agencies are submitting to PPIRS timely performance evaluations on required actions and that these evaluations provide clear, comprehensive, and constructive information that is useful for making future contract award decisions.[4]

B. Mitigating risk of cost-reimbursement and T&M/LH contracts

1. **Be forward leaning in management and oversight of cost-reimbursement and T&M/LH contracts**. The government must ensure contractor costs are reasonable and the contractor is making progress in accordance with the contract's performance schedule. In particular, agencies must:

   - determine that the contractor's accounting system is adequate for determining costs related to the contract. Determinations must be periodically updated. Periodic updates are necessitated by the organizational changes contractors make to keep pace with the dynamic demands of the marketplace.

   - have in place appropriate government surveillance to provide reasonable assurance that efficient methods and effective cost controls are in place. Agencies that rely on invoice reviews by contracting officer technical representatives (COTRs) should ensure the COTRs have the skills and capacity to perform adequate reviews before payment is made to contractors. When cost, schedule, or performance variances are identified, agencies should increase their management attention to ensure such variances are eliminated or otherwise addressed.

2. **Link payment to performance on cost-plus-award-fee contracts**. Risk associated with award fee contracts is high because they are designed for circumstances where requirements may be difficult to define with sufficient specificity to measure objectively. Recent changes to FAR Subpart 16.4 detail the steps agencies are required to take so that risk is managed effectively. These required steps include:

   - determining that an award fee contract is the appropriate contract type;

   - tying fees to cost, timeliness, and quality of the contractor's performance;

   - following prescribed standards for differentiating between levels of performance and the corresponding percentage of available award fee that can be earned; and

---

[4] See OFPP Memorandum, *Improving the Use of Contractor Performance Information* (July 29, 2009), available at http://www.whitehouse.gov/omb/assets/procurement/Improving_the_Use_of_Contractor_Performance_Information.pdf.

- prohibiting both the payment of award fees for unsatisfactory contractor performance and the practice of "roll over" where a contractor is given a second chance to earn fees in a subsequent performance period that were not earned initially.

3. **Determine the appropriateness of T&M/LH contracts in commercial item acquisitions**. Because commercial items have been market tested, risk can be effectively managed in most cases through the use of firm-fixed-price contracts or fixed-price contracts with economic price adjustments. In certain situations, however, such as for emergency repairs, it may not possible at the time of placing the contract to estimate accurately the extent or duration of the work or to anticipate costs with any reasonable degree of confidence. Agencies are authorized to use T&M/LH contracts in these circumstances, but must take care to ensure sufficient analysis underlies the decision, including an explanation of why a fixed-price contract is unsuitable. It is insufficient simply to assert in a D&F that a T&M/LH contract is suitable.[5]

4. **Provide for the necessary skills and capacity in the acquisition workforce to award and manage a cost-type contract**. Development, negotiation, and management of cost-type contracts generally demand more in-depth programmatic knowledge and experience, a higher level and broader range of skills (e.g., including but not limited to, finance, accounting, cost and price analysis, industrial engineering, and program management), and greater resources than are required for competitively awarded fixed-price contracts.

---

[5] A recent GAO review found limited use of D&Fs for commercial item contracts due, in large part, to a general unawareness of the requirement and lack of its express application to the Multiple Award Schedules (MAS) Program. See *CONTRACT MANAGEMENT: Minimal Compliance with New Safeguards for Time-and-Materials Contracts for Commercial Services and Safeguards Have Not Been Applied To GSA Schedules Program*, GAO-09-579 (June 2009). A FAR case has been opened to expressly apply the D&F requirements generally required for commercial item acquisitions to MAS acquisitions and to consider where additional regulatory or other policy guidance may be beneficial, such as in the reinforcement of requirements associated with acquisition planning.

Key Question #3

How is the agency creating opportunities to transition to more competitive or lower risk contracts?

Initial considerations

A. Transitioning to more competitive contracting

1. **Engage the marketplace to determine how barriers to competition can be removed**. Agencies should encourage their contract specialists and program offices to speak to sources, including leading competitors and sources that expressed interest in the procurement (e.g,. responded to a request for information, participated in an industry day, or contacted the agency OSDBU) but ultimately did not submit offers to understand the basis for their decision not to participate. These discussions might reveal, for example, that:

   - the requirements were not sufficiently clear;
   - sufficient time was not provided to the offerors to perform due diligence;
   - requirements were grouped inconsistent with the way services are commonly performed or provided by industry, or otherwise bundled to make it difficult for small businesses to compete.
   - insufficient reliance was placed on commercial standards;
   - criteria that were used to evaluate sources did not permit meaningful comparison and discrimination between and among competing proposals.

   Contract specialists and program officials should ask sources if future plans, such as those described in published justifications and approval documents for sole-source contracts, will be effective in encouraging competition and if other alternatives should be considered.

2. **Do a spend analysis of the agency's largest spend categories**. Spend analysis is a basic tool for agencies to evaluate the strength of their competition practices and identify opportunities for improvement. Spend analysis may be especially useful for identifying and analyzing competitions for which only one offer was received. To accomplish a spend analysis, an agency might use data in the Federal Procurement Data System (FPDS) to identify the agency's largest spending categories to analyze and compare levels of competition achieved by different organizations within the agency or by organizations similarly situated in other agencies to determine if more successful practices may exist for obtaining greater marketplace competition for a given spending category. OFPP and the Competition Working Group of the Chief Acquisition Officers Council will help agencies create competition profiles that can inform the development of goals and plans for increasing competition on a fiscal year basis.

B. Transitioning to lower risk contract types

1. **Use appropriate mechanisms, such as contract review boards, peer reviews, or contract type advocates to bring additional expertise to bear in determining the best contract type**. FAR 16.103(c) cautions contracting officers to avoid protracted use of a cost-reimbursement or T&M/LH contract after experience provides a basis for firmer pricing. The FAR explains that changing circumstances may make a different contract type appropriate in later periods than that used at the outset. Contract review boards and/or peer reviews can facilitate stronger analyses to determine the best contract type. Teams should include not only contracting experts with relevant background but other appropriate officials such as program managers, systems engineers, and other technical personnel. These reviews can produce constructive ideas and alternatives to test whether bases commonly cited to support the use of high risk contract types, such as complexity of the requirements, uncertain duration of the work, or lack of meaningful spend data, exist and, if so, whether reasonable mitigation steps have been taken. For example, a review might:

    *   reveal ways in which complexity and/or uncertainty can be reduced, such as by disaggregating requirements;

    *   ensure steps have been taken to differentiate certain and uncertain requirements so that fixed-price options can be used where requirements are known and not-to-exceed amounts for uncertain requirements can be replaced with fixed-price options over time as a pricing history can be established to support firm pricing; and

    *   help the acquiring organization improve its use of spend data, such as by using standard methodologies for collecting information on costs, so costs incurred on similar projects or subprojects can be compared more easily to create a history that supports fixed-pricing on future procurements involving similar requirements.

    Agency analyses and associated recommendations should be documented in the contract file to help agency officials with subsequent reviews and decision making. If the agency decides that it is premature to transition to a fixed-price contract, the file should explain the rationale for the decision -- for example:

    *   why it remains difficult to define requirements with a reasonable degree of certainty;

    *   what spend data has been collected and analyzed, especially for ongoing work that is the subject of a contract option or renewal, and why it does not support firm-fixed pricing; and

    *   for T&M/LH contracts, why no other contract type is suitable, including cost-reimbursement contracts for acquisitions of non-commercial items.

71

Agencies that rely on high-risk contracting to a significant extent are encouraged to consider designating a contracting official to serve as a dedicated "contract type advocate." This advocate could bring greater attention to internal contract type selection practices not only in choosing between fixed-price, cost-reimbursement, and T&M/LH contracts, but also in selecting the type of incentive that can best motivate strong performance and mitigate risk in different situations.

2. **<u>Award contracts that allow the agency to choose between a fixed-price, cost-reimbursement, or T&M/LH basis for the payment of different contract requirements</u>**. A hybrid contract may allow the agency to achieve a better match between the requirement and how the work is priced. Work for which there is a basis for firm pricing can be awarded for a firm-fixed price while requirements for which there remains considerable uncertainty can be acquired on a cost or T&M/LH basis.[6]

   - An agency undertaking a large-scale project with significant development could use a hybrid contract to pay for studies of early design on a cost or T&M/LH basis, later design and initial development using a cost-plus incentive fee arrangement, and initial and full scale production for a firm-fixed price. Of course, agencies should, whenever possible, employ strategies that encourage up front due diligence so that vendors can come up with lower risk solutions that can be met with fixed-price contracts at the earliest feasible point in the acquisition lifecycle, thereby limiting the need to resort to riskier contracting forms.

   - A hybrid contract might support different types of incentive fees so that an agency may use incentive fee contracts with objective performance metrics whenever requirements can be measured objectively and limit the use of award fee contracts with subjective criteria to those requirements whose outcomes cannot be effectively measured objectively.

A hybrid contract may require additional monitoring to ensure payment is made in accordance with agreed-upon terms (e.g., overruns created by performance inefficiencies on work awarded for a firm-fixed price must not be charged to a cost-reimbursement line item).

---

[6] As an alternative to a hybrid contract, an agency could competitively award a series of contracts addressing smaller increments or modules of work.

APPENDIX B

GOVERNMENT CONTRACTING

Contract Types

THE WHITE HOUSE

Office of the Press Secretary
_____

For Immediate Release   March 4, 2009

Memorandum for the Heads of Executive Departments and Agencies

Subject: Government Contracting

The Federal Government has an overriding obligation to American taxpayers. It should perform its functions efficiently and effectively while ensuring that its actions result in the best value for the taxpayers.

Since 2001, spending on Government contracts has more than doubled, reaching over $500 billion in 2008. During this same period, there has been a significant increase in the dollars awarded without full and open competition and an increase in the dollars obligated through cost-reimbursement contracts. Between fiscal years 2000 and 2008, for example, dollars obligated under cost-reimbursement contracts nearly doubled, from $71 billion in 2000 to $135 billion in 2008. Reversing these trends away from full and open competition and toward cost-reimbursement contracts could result in savings of billions of dollars each year for the American taxpayer.

Excessive reliance by executive agencies on sole-source contracts (or contracts with a limited number of sources) and cost-reimbursement contracts creates a risk that taxpayer funds will be spent on contracts that are wasteful, inefficient, subject to misuse, or otherwise not well designed to serve the needs of the Federal Government or the interests of the American taxpayer. Reports by agency Inspectors General, the Government Accountability Office (GAO), and other independent reviewing bodies have shown that noncompetitive and cost-reimbursement contracts have been misused, resulting in wasted taxpayer resources, poor contractor performance, and inadequate accountability for results.

When awarding Government contracts, the Federal Government must strive for an open and competitive process. However, executive agencies must have the flexibility to tailor contracts to carry out their missions and achieve the policy goals of the Government. In certain exigent circumstances, agencies may need to consider whether a competitive process will not accomplish the agency's mission. In such cases, the agency must ensure that the risks associated with noncompetitive contracts are minimized.

Moreover, it is essential that the Federal Government have the capacity to carry out robust and thorough management and oversight of its contracts in order to achieve programmatic goals, avoid significant overcharges, and curb wasteful spending. A GAO study last year of 95 major defense acquisitions projects found cost overruns of 26 percent, totaling $295 billion over the life of the projects. Improved contract oversight could reduce such sums significantly.

Government outsourcing for services also raises special concerns. For decades, the Federal Government has relied on the private sector for necessary commercial services used by the Government, such as transportation, food, and maintenance. Office of Management and Budget Circular A-76, first issued in 1966, was based on the reasonable premise that while inherently governmental activities should be performed by Government employees, taxpayers may receive more value for their dollars if non-inherently governmental activities that can be provided commercially are subject to the forces of competition.

However, the line between inherently governmental activities that should not be outsourced and commercial activities that may be subject to private sector competition has been blurred and inadequately defined. As a result, contractors may be performing inherently governmental functions. Agencies and departments must operate under clear rules prescribing when outsourcing is and is not appropriate.

It is the policy of the Federal Government that executive agencies shall not engage in noncompetitive contracts except in those circumstances where their use can be fully justified and where appropriate safeguards have been put in place to protect the taxpayer. In addition, there shall be a preference for fixed-price type contracts. Cost-reimbursement contracts shall be used only when circumstances do not allow the agency to define its requirements sufficiently to allow for a fixed-price type contract. Moreover, the Federal Government shall ensure that taxpayer dollars are not spent on contracts that are wasteful, inefficient, subject to misuse, or otherwise not well designed to serve the Federal Government's needs and to manage the risk associated with the goods and services being procured. The Federal Government must have sufficient capacity to manage and oversee the contracting process from start to finish, so as to ensure that taxpayer funds are spent wisely and are not subject to excessive risk. Finally, the Federal Government must ensure that those functions that are inherently governmental in nature are performed by executive agencies and are not outsourced.

I hereby direct the Director of the Office of Management and Budget (OMB), in collaboration with the Secretary of Defense, the Administrator of the National Aeronautics and Space Administration, the Administrator of General Services, the Director of the Office of Personnel Management, and the heads of such other agencies as the Director of OMB determines to be appropriate, and with the participation of appropriate management councils and program management officials, to develop and issue by July 1, 2009, Government-wide guidance to assist agencies in reviewing, and creating processes for ongoing review of, existing contracts in order to identify contracts that are wasteful, inefficient, or not otherwise likely to meet the agency's needs, and to formulate appropriate corrective action in a timely manner. Such corrective action may include modifying or canceling such contracts in a manner and to the extent consistent with applicable laws, regulations, and policy.

I further direct the Director of OMB, in collaboration with the aforementioned officials and councils, and with input from the public, to develop and issue by September 30, 2009, Government-wide guidance to:

1. Govern the appropriate use and oversight of sole-source and other types of noncompetitive contracts and to maximize the use of full and open competition and other competitive procurement processes;

2. Govern the appropriate use and oversight of all contract types, in full consideration of the agency's needs, and to minimize risk and maximize the value of Government contracts generally, consistent with the regulations to be promulgated pursuant to section 864 of Public Law 110-417;

3. Assist agencies in assessing the capacity and ability of the Federal acquisition workforce to develop, manage, and oversee acquisitions appropriately; and

4. Clarify when governmental outsourcing for services is and is not appropriate, consistent with section 321 of Public Law 110-417 (31 U.S.C. 501 note).

Executive departments and agencies shall carry out the provisions of this memorandum to the extent permitted by law. This memorandum is not intended to, and does not, create any right or benefit, substantive or procedural, enforceable at law or in equity by any party against the United States, its departments, agencies, or entities, its officers, employees, or agents, or any other person.

The Director of OMB is hereby authorized and directed to publish this memorandum in the *Federal Register.*

BARACK OBAMA

# # #

APPENDIX C

IMPROVING GOVERNMENT ACQUISITION

THE DIRECTOR

EXECUTIVE OFFICE OF THE PRESIDENT
OFFICE OF MANAGEMENT AND BUDGET
WASHINGTON, D.C. 20503

July 29, 2009

M-09-25

MEMORANDUM FOR THE HEADS OF DEPARTMENTS AND AGENCIES

FROM: Peter R. Orszag
                    Director

SUBJECT: Improving Government Acquisition

The President's Memorandum on Government Contracting, issued on March 4, 2009, calls on federal agencies to improve the effectiveness of their acquisition practices and the results achieved from their contracts. Sound acquisition practices help agencies guard against inefficiency and waste and improve their ability to obtain quality supplies and services that are on time and within budget.

The Presidential Memorandum requires OMB to issue guidance in two steps. The first step, presented here, is guidance on reviewing existing contracts and acquisition practices. The second, due in the fall, is guidance on competition, contract types, acquisition workforce, and outsourcing. Closely-related additional guidance, on managing the multi-sector workforce and on holding contractors accountable for past performance, is being issued concurrently with this guidance.

This memorandum requires agencies to take the following actions: (1) review their existing contracts and acquisition practices and develop a plan to save 7 percent of baseline contract spending by the end of FY 2011; and (2) reduce by 10 percent the share of dollars obligated in FY 2010 under new contract actions that are awarded with high-risk contracting authorities.

I. Acquisition savings plans

The Administration has set a net savings target of $40 billion a year through better acquisition and acquisition-related program practices. Accordingly, each agency shall develop a plan to save 3.5 percent of baseline contract spending in FY 2010 and a further 3.5 percent in FY 2011. These savings may be used to meet the budget targets in OMB's June 11, 2009 guidance on FY 2011 budget submissions. The plan should identify the steps that will be taken along with the projected savings for each identified step. Agencies that have recently announced or commenced acquisition reforms may count the savings from these reforms in meeting the 7 percent target.

There are many ways in which an agency may achieve savings from their acquisition activities. For example, savings can be realized by: (1) ending contracts that do not meet program needs or projects that are no longer needed, (2) building the skills of the acquisition workforce and recruiting new talent so as to negotiate more favorably priced contracts and manage contract costs more effectively, (3) developing more strategic acquisition approaches to leverage buying power and achieve best value for the taxpayer, (4) increasing the use of technology to improve contract management, and (5) reengineering ineffective business processes and practices to reduce cost to spend. A further description of some of these steps is provided in Attachment 1.

The specific actions agencies take will vary based on how the agency currently uses contracting to support its mission, its human capital and technology requirements, and the current quality and effectiveness of its acquisition processes and practices. Accordingly, each agency must identify and prioritize its particular needs and develop a tailored plan to improve the performance and cost-effectiveness of its acquisition activities.

II. Reducing the use of high risk contracting authorities

Noncompetitive contracting, cost-reimbursement contracts, and time-and-materials and labor-hour (T&M/LH) contracts pose special risks of overspending. Non-competitive contracts present a risk because there is not a direct market mechanism for setting the contract price. Cost-reimbursement contracts and T&M/LH contracts pose a risk because they provide no direct incentive to the contractor for cost control. While these contract authorities are important tools when used appropriately, reports from the Government Accountability Office (GAO), agency inspectors general, and agency management indicate that they are often used without an appropriate basis or sufficient management and oversight to limit taxpayer risk.

Accordingly, agencies should begin taking actions to reduce use of these high risk contracting authorities for new contract actions. Using FY 2008 achievements as a baseline, agencies should aim to reduce by at least 10 percent the combined share of dollars obligated through new contracts in FY 2010 that are: (1) awarded noncompetitively and/or receive only one bid in response to a solicitation or a request for quote, (2) cost-reimbursement contracts or (3) T&M/LH contracts.

Agencies that wish to address other high-risk authorities should confer with OMB's Office of Federal Procurement Policy. Additional background and information on this request is provided in Attachment 2.

Agencies that are subject to the Chief Financial Officers Act shall develop plans in accordance with this memorandum and submit them to OMB by November 2, 2009. Other agencies are encouraged to consult with OMB and take appropriate steps tailored to their mission needs and operating environments.

Thank you for your attention to this matter.

Attachments

Examples of Steps Agencies Should Consider in Achieving Savings Targets

The following are a few examples of ways an agency might achieve its acquisition savings targets. The approaches described below are of two general types: (A) those that directly reduce spending as a result of decisions which are typically made at the program or project level (e.g., the program's objectives have been accomplished or changed), and (B) those that create savings through more effective acquisition practices. Agencies should develop specific plans that reflect their particular needs and are encouraged to pursue other actions needed to achieve their savings targets.

A. Saving through reductions in spending

- End contracts that are (i) ineffective, (ii) wasteful, (iii) support programs that are being terminated, reduced, or changed in scope, or (iv) not otherwise likely to meet the agency's needs. Agencies should have procedures in place that allow them to review contracts at appropriate decision points, and to evaluate the effectiveness of existing contracts through collaborations between acquisition, program, and project officials, so as to make the most informed decisions about whether to exercise options, renew contracts, or cancel contracts.

Examples:

The Department of Energy projects $30 million in savings in FY 2010 from a proposal, included in the FY 2010 Budget, to terminate funding for a contract to refurbish the Los Alamos Neutron Science Center. This center was built 30 years ago and no longer plays a critical role in weapons research. Maintaining the Center would be cost prohibitive.

The Department of Agriculture projects $18 million in savings in FY 2010 from a planned contract termination that would be made in connection with a proposal, included in the FY 2010 Budget, to end funding for the Watershed and Flood Prevention Operations Program. This program has a lower economic return than other Federal flood prevention programs and more than 95 percent of the program was earmarked in FY 2009, which has undermined the Department's ability to use project evaluations as a basis for prioritizing funding.

Agencies are encouraged to review the alignment between their acquisition, project, and program activities. The effective integration of these activities lies at the heart of an agency's ability to achieve desired cost, schedule, and performance outcomes from programs that rely significantly on contractors to provide supplies and services. OMB's Office of Federal Procurement Policy (OFPP) will post a reference document at http://www.whitehouse.gov/omb/procurement_default/ that agencies can use, as appropriate, to evaluate where opportunities for improved alignment in agency activities may exist.

B. Savings through more effective acquisition practices

- <u>Strengthen the acquisition workforce</u>. Agencies should analyze whether the current size, skill-level, and organizational structure of their acquisition workforces are sufficient to achieve a high performance level. As appropriate, agencies should develop plans to (a) increase the size of their acquisition workforce (broadly defined to include contracting, program management, and the contracting officer's technical representative), (b) make any necessary investments in training, and (c) restructure acquisition workflows to improve efficiency and free up acquisition workforce time for more strategic activities. In analyzing acquisition workforce needs, agencies should pay particular attention to retirement and other separation trends, steps that can be taken to increase retention of experienced acquisition experts, and ways to emphasize the importance of acquisition work as a high-prestige management responsibility critical to agency mission success. Agencies are encouraged to provide specific information on the additional FTEs and funding necessary to carry out their proposed plan for strengthening the acquisition function.

- <u>Strengthen acquisition practices</u>. Agencies should review their acquisition practices and compare them to best practices at other agencies. Practices that have been shown to improve acquisition outcomes include:

  o enhancing upfront planning to align program requirements and acquisition strategies and to make sure acquisition requirements are clearly specified;

  o increasing the amount of attention paid to market analysis, cost estimates, and choice of contract types and incentives, so as to achieve excellent and cost effective performance;

  o increasing the amount of attention paid early in the acquisition process to ensuring that sufficient internal capacity is or will be in place to effectively manage and oversee contract performance and mitigate risks after award;

  o instituting peer reviews at critical stages of high-priority acquisitions to bring the agency's best expertise to bear to ensure effective execution of acquisition, project, and program responsibilities. Peer reviews can be conducted in a variety of ways, but typically evaluate if an acquisition for carrying out the investment is being planned or managed effectively and offer constructive ideas and alternatives for achieving desired outcomes; and

  o ensuring that systems are in place to review contract cost, schedule, and performance goals on an ongoing basis and that corrective actions are taken in a timely manner to affect contract outcomes when variances from these goals occur.

- <u>Develop more strategic acquisition strategies</u>. Agencies should increase their participation in government-wide strategic acquisition initiatives, including strategic sourcing initiatives that reduce costs for all agencies by leveraging the government's buying power and, where appropriate, expand their use of enterprise-wise strategic acquisition initiatives that offer significant savings opportunities from both business process improvements and access to lower product and service costs.

Contract Types

Managing Risk in Noncompetitive, Cost-Reimbursement
and Time-and-Materials and Labor-Hour Contracts

Noncompetitive, cost-reimbursement, and time-and-materials and labor-hour (T&M/LH) contracts play an important role in helping agencies meet needs that arise in a variety of challenging circumstances. Noncompetitive contracts enable agencies to address requirements that can only be satisfied by one source or that arise during emergencies when time allows for only limited consideration of offers. Cost reimbursement contracts help agencies obtain critical research, leading edge innovation, and other needs where there is considerable uncertainty about the resources that will be necessary to achieve the government's objective. T&M/LH contracts help agencies accomplish tasks for a reasonable cost where the needed amount of labor effort cannot be specified in advance, such as when an information technology office must diagnose the cause of a system failure.

Notwithstanding these benefits, each of these authorities carries significant risk of overspending. Noncompetitive contracts force agencies to negotiate contracts without the benefit of a direct market mechanism to help establish pricing. Cost-reimbursement and T&M/LH contracts provide limited incentive to control costs. However, by recognizing and managing these risks, agencies can avoid wasteful spending and meet needs under conditions where other acquisition strategies are likely to be less effective.

Accordingly, agencies are encouraged to review the adequacy and effectiveness of their internal procedures and practices related to the use of these vehicles and make improvements where weaknesses are identified. Good stewardship might include:

- Applying additional resources to the analysis and negotiation of fair and reasonable prices for noncompetitive contracts, examining the reasons why only one offer was received in response to a solicitation to ensure the government is not engaging in restrictive practices that reduce competition, and working with requirements officials to explore opportunities for new solutions that might be met by two or more sources;

- Planning for the migration of work from a cost-type to fixed-price contract as requirements become better defined; and

- Performing an analysis of organizations within the agency that have repeatedly renewed T&M/LH contracts to consider the continued need and cost-effectiveness of such arrangements, whether other contract types are more suited, and if in-sourcing should be considered, either because the agency has insufficient internal capability to manage its operations or might save costs by converting the work to federal performance.

In addition to mitigating risks when these contract authorities are employed, agencies should make sure to limit use of these authorities to situations when they are truly appropriate. Reports from the Government Accountability Office, agency inspectors general, and agency management point to a general overuse of these authorities that requires agency action – specifically, a reduction in use for new contract actions. Therefore, this guidance calls for agencies to reduce by at least 10 percent the combined share of dollars obligated through new contracts in FY 2010 that are (1) awarded noncompetitively and/or receive only one bid in response to a solicitation or a request for quote, (2) cost-reimbursement contracts, or (3) T&M/LH contracts.

Thus, an agency that in FY 2008 had 40 percent of its contract dollars in these high-risk categories should reduce this number to at most 36 percent of the dollars obligated through new contract actions in FY 2010.

Noncompetitive awards include, at a minimum, those otherwise subject to competition under Part 6 of the Federal Acquisition Regulation (FAR) that were not competed on the basis that there is only one responsible source (i.e., FAR 6.302-1) or unusual and compelling urgency (i.e., 6.302-2). In defining the class of contracts targeted for reduction, agencies are encouraged to include also awards made pursuant to FAR 8.405-6, which authorizes agencies to restrict their consideration of contractors under the Federal Supply Schedules program, and (2) FAR 16.505(b)(2), which permits agencies to make awards under a multiple award contract without giving fair opportunity to all contract holders.[1]

As a result of reviewing internal practices, agencies may identify additional high-risk activities in need of management attention. Agencies that wish to address other high-risk authorities as part of their target should consult with OFPP.

Other efforts

Changes will soon be made in the FAR to improve policies and practices associated with the use of cost-reimbursement contracting and help to guard against their overuse. Consistent with section 864 of Public Law 110-417, these changes will address: (1) when and under what circumstances cost-reimbursement contracts are appropriate, (2) the acquisition plan findings necessary to support a decision to use cost-reimbursement contracts, and (3) the acquisition workforce resources necessary to award and manage cost-reimbursement contracts.

OFPP is also working on guidance with agency Chief Acquisition Officers to further strengthen use of competition and selection of contract type. The guidance will be issued later this fall, in accordance with the President's Memorandum on Government Contracting.

---

[1] Agencies should not include acquisitions in their target that are made noncompetitively pursuant to a statute that authorizes or requires that the acquisition be made through another agency or from a specified source, including those identified in FAR 6.302-5(b), such as sole source awards made under the small business development "8(a)" program, the HUBZone Act, or the Veterans Benefits Act, awards made to qualified nonprofit agencies for the blind or other severely disabled pursuant to the Javits-Wagner-O'Day Act, and awards made to Federal Prison Industries pursuant to 18 U.S.C. 4124. In addition, agencies need not, as a general matter, address actions in their target that are made pursuant to FAR 6.302-3,-4, -6, or -7.

APPENDIX D

Award Fee Contracts (FAR 16, DFARS 215, DFARS 216)

Contract Types

Subject: Award Fee Contracts (FAR 16, DFARS 215, DFARS 216).

Title Annotation:	*Policy & Legislation*
Author:	*Finley, James I.*
Date:	*July 1, 2006*
Words:	*834*
Publication:	*Defense AT & L*
ISSN:	*1547-5476*

OFFICE OF THE UNDER SECRETARY OF DEFENSE
3000 DEFENSE PENTAGON
WASHINGTON, DC 20301-3000
MAR 29 2006
[ILLUSTRATION OMITTED]
MEMORANDUM FOR SECRETARIES OF THE MILITARY DEPARTMENTS ATTN: ACQUISITION
EXECUTIVES DIRECTORS OF THE DEFENSE AGENCIES

SUBJECT: Award Fee Contracts (FAR 16, DFARS 215, DFARS 216)

Award fee contracts must be structured in ways that will focus the government's and contractor's efforts on meeting or exceeding cost, schedule, and performance requirements. The ability to earn award fees needs to be directly linked to achieving desired program outcomes. In December 2005, the Government Accountability Office (GAO) issued a report entitled "DEFENSE ACQUISITIONS: DoD Has Paid Billions in Award and Incentive Fees Regardless of Acquisition Outcomes" <http://www.gao.gov/new.items/d0666.pdf>, which made a number of recommendations on how to improve the use of award fees.

In the DoD response dated December 12, 2005, the Department generally concurred with the recommendations in the report and agreed to issue a policy memo by March 31,2006, to (1) address desired outcomes and the role the award fee should play in the overall acquisition strategy; (2) remind the acquisition workforce to follow existing policies; (3) provide guidance to the acquisition workforce on "rollover"; and (4) develop a communication plan to share proven incentive strategies across the entire DoD acquisition workforce. These actions correspond to Recommendations 1, 2, 4 and 7, respectively, in the GAO report. Separately, the Department will respond to Recommendations 3, 5 and 6 of the report at a later time. While award fee contracts are intended to be flexible, this memorandum provides additional guidance on the proper use of award fees.

Link Award Fees to Desired Outcomes (GAO Recommendation 1)

Award Fee Contracts (FAR 16, DFARS 215, DFARS 216)

While award fee contracts are used when it is neither feasible nor effective to devise predetermined objective performance targets, it is imperative that award fees be tied to identifiable interim outcomes, discrete events or milestones, as much as possible. Examples of such interim milestones include timely completion of preliminary design review, critical design review, and successful system demonstration. In situations where there may be no identifiable milestone for a year or more, consideration should be given to apportioning some of the award fee pool for a predetermined interim period of time based on assessing progress toward milestones. In any case, award fee provisions must clearly explain how a contractor's performance will be evaluated.

Award Fees Must Be Commensurate with Contractor Performance (GAO Recommendation 2)

While award fee arrangements should be structured to motivate excellent contractor performance, award fees must be commensurate with contractor performance over a range from satisfactory to excellent performance. Clearly, satisfactory performance should earn considerably less than excellent performance, otherwise the motivation to achieve excellence is negated. However, because base fees are typically limited to no more than three percent of target cost (DFARS 216.405-2), it is appropriate to award a portion of the award fee pool for satisfactory performance to ensure that contractors receive an adequate fee on our contracts. Performance that is less than satisfactory is not entitled to any award fee.

Rollover of Award Fees (GAO Recommendation 4)

An element of many award fee plans is the ability to "roll over" unearned award fee money from one period to another. The following limitations on the use of "rollover" are established:

- Use of a "rollover" provision should be the exception rather than the rule.

- Use of an award fee rollover provision is a business decision and should be addressed in the acquisition strategy, including the rationale as to why a rollover provision is appropriate.

- If "rollover" is used, the contractor may only earn a portion of the fee that was rolled over, even for subsequent excellent performance. Factors to consider in determining how much to reduce the available rollover fee include how close the contractor came to meeting the scheduled milestone in terms of cost, schedule, and performance. For example, the reduction in rollover fees for missing a milestone by a year should be significantly greater than for missing a milestone by 30 days.

- If the Fee Determining Official approves the use of "rollover," the official contract file must be documented accordingly and the contractor must be notified.

Communication Plan (GAO Recommendation 7)

In order to facilitate discussion and to share proven incentive strategies across the entire acquisition workforce, the Department has established the "Award and Incentive Fees" Community of Practice (CoP) under the leadership of the Defense Acquisition University (DAU). The CoP will serve as the repository for all related materials including policy information, related training courses, examples of good award fee arrangements, and other supporting resources related to this policy memorandum. The CoP is available on the DAU Acquisition Community Connection at <https://acc.dau.mil/awardandincentivefees>.

This policy memorandum is effective immediately. The DFARS and/or its PGI supplement will be revised to reflect the policy contents of this memorandum. Please direct any questions to Michael Canales at 703-695-8571 or e-mail Michael.Canales@osd.mil.

James I. Finley
Deputy Under Secretary of Defense (Acquisition and Technology)

APPENDIX E

Appropriate Use of Incentive Contracts

Contract Types

EXECUTIVE OFFICE OF THE PRESIDENT
OFFICE OF MANAGEMENT AND BUDGET
WASHINGTON, D.C. 20503
OFFICE OF FEDERAL
PROCUREMENT POLICY

December 4, 2007

MEMORANDUM FOR CHIEF ACQUISITION OFFICERS

SENIOR PROCUREMENT EXECUTIVES

FROM: Paul A. Denett
Administrator

SUBJECT: Appropriate Use of Incentive Contracts

Incentive contracts are used throughout the Federal Government to encourage contractors to perform efficiently and effectively. Using incentives appropriately and applying strong project and acquisition management practices are vital to accomplishing mission needs, minimizing waste, and maximizing value. The purpose of this memorandum is to request your assistance and leadership to ensure incentive fee contracts are used to motivate excellent contractor performance. Specifically, please review your agency's acquisition policies to ensure that: 1) incentive fees are linked to acquisition outcomes such as cost, schedule, and performance results; and 2) incentive fees are not earned if the contractor's performance is judged to be below satisfactory or does not meet the basic requirements of the contract.

The Federal Acquisition Regulation (FAR) states that incentive fee contracts, which include award fee contracts, should be used to achieve specific performance objectives established prior to contract award, such as delivering products and services on time, within cost goals, and with promised performance outcomes. Awards must be tied to demonstrated results, as opposed to effort, in meeting or exceeding specified performance standards.

Recently, the Government Accountability Office (GAO) identified programs and supporting contracts in which incentive fee payment practices did not result in achievement of contract objectives. GAO identified the following practices that reduce the effectiveness of fees as a motivational tool: 1) evaluating contractors on incentive criteria that are not directly related to cost, schedule, and performance goals; 2) paying contractors a significant portion of the available fee for what is considered acceptable or satisfactory performance; and 3) giving contractors additional opportunities to obtain initially unearned fees, also known as rollover fees.

As part of acquisition planning, when determining whether to use incentive fee contracts, the contracting officer should conduct risk and cost benefit analyses. Contract type is generally determined based on a consideration of risk to the government and the contractor. In addition to risk, cost benefit analyses related to use of incentive contracts should consider the amount of planning required to implement an incentive type contract and the amount of additional resources required for monitoring and determining awards. Risk and cost analyses related to the use of award and incentive contracts should be prepared in writing and approved at a level above the contracting officer or as determined by the agency.

Incentive fees must be predetermined in writing and processes for awarding the fees must be included or cross-referenced in the acquisition plan (see FAR 7.105(b)(4)(i)). This incentive fee plan should include standards for evaluating contractor performance and appropriate incentive fee amounts. When considering the incentive fee arrangement, the plan should distinguish between earning potential for satisfactory versus excellent performance. Metrics should clearly describe what is required and at what point a contractor is considered successful. Additionally, agencies should develop guidance on when it is appropriate to award rollovers of unearned fee to a subsequent evaluation period. Rolling over fees is not the preferred method for incentivizing the contractor to perform above satisfactorily and should be permitted on a limited basis and require prior approval of the appropriate agency official.

Using the attachment as a guide, Chief Acquisition Officers should review and update existing agency guidance on incentive fee contracting practices to ensure that fees are awarded in accordance with current regulations and that the guidance addresses the concerns of this memorandum. In addition, during an agency's internal audit process, incentive fee contracts should be reviewed as part of the program management review process. Information on how well incentive fees are achieving their intended purpose and other related lessons learned can be found and shared on the Acquisition Community Connection on https://acc.dau.mil/CommunityBrowser. aspx?id=105550&lang=en-US.

To help develop best practices, guidance, and templates, OFPP requests that agencies identify an incentive and award fee point of contact. These individuals may be asked to contribute examples and lessons learned to an interagency working group or to assist in communication and awareness efforts. Please submit the person's name, title, telephone number, and e-mail address to Susan Truslow at OFPP by January 7, 2008.

Please ensure broad dissemination of this memorandum among agency personnel who have responsibilities for the effective planning, execution, and management of your acquisitions. Questions may be referred to Susan Truslow at (202) 395-6810 or struslow@omb.eop.gov or Pat Corrigan at (202) 395-6805 or pcorrigan@omb. eop.gov .

Thank you for your attention to this important matter.

Attachment

cc: Chief Information Officers

Contract Types

Attachment

Incentive Contract Checklist

- Consult agency policy and guidance that supplement FAR 16.4, Incentive Contracts.

- Ensure market research documentation and the acquisition plan sufficiently state desired outcomes, performance requirements, milestones, risks and cost benefits associated with choice of contract type (FAR 7.105).

- Conduct and document risk and cost/benefit analyses that support use of an incentive type contract:

  - Conduct a risk assessment and ensure incentive strategies are consistent with the level of risk assumed by the contractor and motivate the contractor by balancing awards with negative consequences;

  - Determine whether administrative costs associated with managing the incentive fee are outweighed by the expected benefits; and

  - Ensure sufficient human resources are available to properly structure and monitor the contract.

- Ensure evaluation factors are:

  - Meaningful and measurable;

  - Directly linked to cost, schedule, and performance results; and

- Designed to motivate excellence in contractor performance by making clear distinctions in possible award earnings between satisfactory and excellent performance.

- Ensure the incentive fee plan:

  - Defines clearly the standards of performance for each rating category (e.g., satisfactory, above satisfactory, excellent);

  - Defines clearly the percentage of fee the contractor should be paid for each of these rating categories;

  - Documents roles and responsibilities for those involved in monitoring contractor performance and determining award fees;

  - Provides detailed guidance on steps in the evaluation process for agency representatives and contractors;

  - Establishes a base fee. Good business practice allows the contractor more than 0% for base fee. This way, the award fee promotes above average performance; and

  - Obtains appropriate approval in accordance with agency policy.

- Ensure rollover fees are allowed only in limited circumstances in accordance with agency policy.